Advance Praise for *There Are No Overachievers*

"Every moment is both a gift and an opportunity. The secret to living life fully is to seize those 'windows of opportunity,' or WOOS, as Brian Biro calls them in his inspiring new book, *There Are No Overachievers*. Brian helps all of us to recognize and act upon the WOOs that lead us to lives of joy, fulfillment, and richness, and allow our light to shine!"

—Nido R. Qubein, president of High Point University

"Over the years, I've read hundreds of leadership books, but *There Are No Overachievers* stands alone. It's an insightful and astute guide on how to be your very best at home and at work. Although I've been fortunate to enjoy great success in my career overall, there are so many times that I missed my window of opportunity to positively impact others' lives. I was too easy to offend and hard to impress. Brian Biro is a life-changer. I enthusiastically recommend this book. It will bring you closer to your colleagues, your friends, and your loved ones."

—Naomi Cramer, senior vice president and chief HR officer of Banner Health

"The energy and pure magic that Brian Biro brings to any situation is life-changing, and he has captured that quality brilliantly in his new book, *There Are No Overachievers*. His motivational messages will impact everyone, from entry-level employees to the upper echelon of management professionals."

—Chris Cicchinelli, president and CEO of Pure Romance

"A masterful presentation of simple yet transformational principles that can be used immediately to enhance relationships and careers. When you read *There Are No Overachievers*, you will begin looking at your life through a new lens of passion, gratitude, and service."

—John Locke, master networker

"The answer is YES! Now what's the question? This is Brian Biro in one sentence. Positive approaches create trust. I have known and worked with Brian for over twenty years. This extraordinary book provides all the lessons that one needs to be successful and, most important, fulfilled at what they do."

—Keith D. Paglusch, CTO of C Spire

"Seeing Brian live is always a treat, but reading *There Are No Overachievers* is like having Brian with me every day. The chapter called 'Be Easy to Impress and Hard to Offend' really struck a chord in me. Look for ways to be impressed, and instead of taking offense at criticism you encounter, transform negative feedback into ways to improve, exceed expectations, and generate loyalty. It is at the heart of everything our company is about and has helped us build the largest global sourcing association in the world. My copy is dog-eared already; I will be referring to it for years to come."

—Dawn Tiura, CEO of SIG: The Executive Sourcing Network

"You will emerge from this book with more confidence, energy, and passion than you've ever imagined for your career, your family, and your life. In a world so often focused on obstacles and barriers, Brian Biro brings fresh light to our possibilities, strengths, and breakthrough potential!"

—Melissa Brisbois, executive vice president of J. Hilburn

"The inspiration and stories in *There Are No Overachievers* opened my eyes to the many 'windows of opportunity' that can help me make a positive difference. It has ignited my own energy and purpose to live this journey called life with more JOY!"

—Dana. L. Stonestreet, bank chairman, president, and CEO of HomeTrust

"Phenomenal! Brian Biro offers us a clear path to increased personal performance and greater success in every area of our lives. And what we get along the way is the life we've always wanted."

—Dr. John B. Waterhouse, former president and field leader of Centers for Spiritual Living

THERE ARE *NO* OVERACHIEVERS

Seizing Your

Windows of Opportunity

to Do More Than

You Thought Possible

BRIAN D. BIRO

CROWN
BUSINESS
NEW YORK

Crown Business books are available at special discounts for bulk
purchases for sales promotions or corporate use. Special editions,
including personalized covers, excerpts of existing books, or
books with corporate logos, can be created in large quantities for
special needs. For more information, contact Premium Sales at
(212) 572-2232 or email specialmarkets@penguinrandomhouse.com.

Library of Congress Cataloging-in-Publication Data
Names: Biro, Brian D., author.
Title: There are no overachievers : seizing your windows of
opportunity to do more than you thought possible / Brian D. Biro.
Description: New York : Crown Business, 2017.
Identifiers: LCCN 2016027868 | ISBN 9780451497628 (hardback)
Subjects: LCSH: Success. | Success in business. | Self-realization. |
BISAC: BUSINESS & ECONOMICS / Motivational. | BUSINESS &
ECONOMICS / Management.
Classification: LCC BF637.S8 B493 2017 | DDC 650.1—dc23
LC record available at https://lccn.loc.gov/2016027868

ISBN 978-0-451-49762-8
Ebook ISBN 978-0-451-49764-2

Printed in the United States of America

Jacket illustration: Francesco Bongiorni

10 9 8 7 6 5 4 3 2 1

First Edition

Every breath I take, every word I write, and every presentation I deliver are inspired by the three greatest lights in my life: my wife, Carole, and daughters Kelsey and Jenna. There is more brilliance, beauty, joy, and strength in each of you than you've ever dreamed possible. Thank you for filling me with passion and purpose. You make every day an exciting WOO!

CONTENTS

Contents

I will never forget my first opportunity to sit down and talk with the legendary college basketball coach John Wooden. At the time I was the vice president and general manager of a large training company in San Diego that specialized in delivering leadership and team-building seminars throughout North America. I had grown up in Southern California and was a huge fan of Coach Wooden and UCLA basketball. But as great as his teams at UCLA were—he won ten NCAA championships in his years coaching there—it was his kindness, his humility, and the dignity and respect with which he treated everyone around him that I admired most.

Having looked up to Coach Wooden for so long, I thought it would be inspiring to share his principles and insights with my own team of leaders. So I phoned Coach Wooden and explained what I had in mind. He invited me to his apartment so I could interview him face-to-face. I was on cloud nine.

To this day, the pearls of wisdom I heard from him that afternoon are indelibly imprinted in my mind and my spirit. Looking at me with a gleam in his eye, he told me, "It's what you learn after you know everything that makes the difference." Given my own fierce conviction about unselfishness and teamwork, I felt like breaking out into a cheer when he told me, "It's amazing what's accomplished when no one cares who gets the credit." But one statement that afternoon struck me more deeply than any other. I asked him what he thought the difference was between good athletes and great ones, between strong performers and those who excelled. He said: "There are no overachievers. We are all underachievers. Very rarely do we even *approach* the greatness that God has given us."

In other words, we *all* have more in us than we think. We can accomplish more, give more, and *be* more than we think is possible personally and professionally. That potential already lies within us.

That simple, profound idea has become a driving force in my life as a husband, father, speaker, and author. Since we already have within us the potential to be more and do more than we ever thought possible, what is holding us back? What are the keys, the secrets, that can lift us personally and professionally to new heights? Ever since that first conversation with Coach Wooden—we got together many times afterward, and he would go on to become my mentor—I have been inspired to discover those answers and help others rise closer to their potential.

I wrote *There Are No Overachievers* to help you discover the greatness within you and build the "maybe I *can*" spirit. Maybe I *can* be a great parent. Maybe I *can* overcome my fear of public speaking. Maybe I *can* become an outstanding leader and lift everyone around me to new heights. Maybe I *can* build a successful business and a terrific career. Maybe I *can* make a difference!

It's time to break through the barriers we create in our lives.

It's time to disrupt the status quo. It's time to break through the comfort zones that so often become confinement zones. It's time to consciously choose happiness, purpose, and possibility over doubt, worry, limitation, and fear. When you do, you'll generate the momentum and energy that will bring you closer to your true potential. Remember, there is greatness within each one of us. Why not set it free?

The Greatest Gift We're Given Is Today!

I am so incredibly blessed! For well over two decades I've had the privilege and opportunity to speak from the stage to more than half a million people around the world about their possibilities, choices, and potential breakthroughs. I've been given the chance to positively impact such leading organizations as Microsoft Worldwide Operations, Lockheed Martin, Kaiser Permanente, Starbucks, Southwest Airlines, PricewaterhouseCoopers, Allstate, Verizon, Boeing, and hundreds of others. Regardless of whether I'm presenting to executive teams, sales, customer service, operations, engineers, or recruits, whenever I talk about my work as a professional speaker I simply can't help but say, "I love what I do. With a passion!" I'll bet I've said that a thousand times.

What surprises and saddens me, however, is how often my expression is met with a look of longing and defeat. "You are so lucky! I wish I felt that way. Do you know how rare it is for someone to feel that way about their work?" I'm told.

The funny thing is, if you had asked me how I felt about my

work when I was in my two previous careers, first as a swimming coach and then as a corporate vice president in the transportation industry, I would have said the same thing: "I love what I do with a passion!" In the years I spent in those professions I hopped out of bed each morning with unstoppable energy and unbridled enthusiasm. When I look back now, I see clearly that the magical ingredient that has always fueled my energy is the passion I have for helping people seize opportunities rather than miss them. It is the ultimate secret required to discover our greatness.

Every day we are given an incredible gift, which I call the WOO. WOO stands for *window of opportunity*—precious, unrepeatable moments that can impact, redirect, and even reshape our lives if we recognize and choose to seize them. WOOs may come into our lives at any moment. In fact, we all share the most magical, exciting, and important of all WOOs right now. The greatest WOO, right there in front of us, is called *today.* It is every precious moment.

You never know if the next person you meet today may become your lifelong friend, just as you didn't know it when you met your current lifelong friends. You never know if the next things you say to your son, daughter, spouse, partner, colleague, friend, employee, or teammate may have so much impact on their lives that their futures shoot off in a whole new trajectory because you helped them see what they couldn't see with their own eyes. You never know if the next idea that pops into your head or the next choice you make may change your life. The important questions to ask yourself now are "How can I recognize a WOO when I see one?" and "Why have I missed WOOs in the past?"

When you seize WOOs you shake your future, energize and engage everyone you touch, build people, teams, and relationships, strengthen your interactions with others, and ultimately create exciting breakthrough results in your life, both personally and professionally. When you do this consistently you become a shining model of personal excellence, integrity, accountability, and humility.

I want to show you how you can seize more WOOs rather than miss them. In the long run this is the ultimate secret to a rich and dynamic life, a successful and fulfilling career, and relationships that bring you inexpressible joy. Is this a promise? WOO yes!

STAGE ONE

SHAKING THE FUTURE

1

Shake Your Future

One evening my wife and daughters and I were dining in a café in the Bitterroot Valley of Montana, where we lived at the time. The café was on the second floor of an old Main Street brick building and had huge windows that captured the stunning panorama of the Bitterroot and Sapphire mountain ranges enclosing our valley. Everyone in the café was eating or chatting quietly when something caught my four-year-old daughter Jenna's attention and she walked over to the window. As she gazed out at the mountains a look of pure wonder came over her, and with great excitement and considerable volume she burst out: "Look, Mommy, Daddy, Kelsey . . . we're in *heaven!*"

Well, the whole place went dead quiet. Everyone stared at us, and we turned bright red. Then after a moment the shock gave way to delight, and grins and laughter erupted all around us at the unbridled joy of Jenna's revelation.

Six months later as I sat in the window seat on my flight to Seattle I looked down at the magnificent puffy cloud formations below me. For some reason the sight made me think of heaven again, which in turn reminded me of Jenna at that café. Grinning, I thought, *My daughter is the cutest kid on the planet!*

But then something hit me like a thunderbolt. Suddenly right there in that plane I saw for the first time that my little girl was *brilliant*. She was a visionary. Why? Because she was the only one who saw heaven. It was right there in front of us, but all I saw was my to-do list, my schedule, and my trials and tribulations. At that moment I decided to put on Jenna's lenses and look for the heaven in everything around me . . . especially in people!

Most of us have never been taught to look at our lives as shining windows of opportunity, or WOOs. In fact, we are powerfully conditioned to do precisely the opposite. In our first five years of life we hear one word more than any other. Though completely well-intentioned, that word is *no*. Our parents love us and want to keep us safe and protected. Instinctively they teach us to be on the lookout for danger and uncertainty, so we develop caution and wariness about the unknown. This is important and vital to our well-being as we experience the complex and fascinating world outside the womb. But over time, two other tremendously powerful words become imprinted in our subconscious as a result, and begin to color the way we view the world. Those words are *or else*: "You better watch out, or else something bad will happen." Then there's another set of words that can slam the brakes on any risk taking: "Be careful or you'll get hurt."

It is easy to assume that as we get older and more experienced we will stop focusing on obstacles, fears, and doubts. But for most of us this is not the case. When parents joke about their children not coming into the world with an instruction manual, they are on to something important. We are not taught to shift our focus toward windows of opportunity. The wariness we learned as children becomes entrenched in our subconscious as we focus more and more on what could go wrong, rather than envisioning what could go right.

How much of the news that we watch on television or read online is positive, energizing, and uplifting? Instead we are bombarded with impending disasters. We worry about our health, our finances, our children, our security, and most of all the unknown and unexpected new obstacles lying in wait around the next corner. Why do we do this? What do we get out of spiraling downward into worst-case scenarios?

But what if there was another way to view each day? What if we were taught a simple, gracious, and enlivening way to begin our day by appreciating it as the greatest gift we are given? What if we were taught to break the pattern of fearing uncertainty and obstacles? What if we replace all of that with the conviction that windows of opportunity are all around us if we look for and open them? What if we broke through the status quo and learned that *happiness is a choice*? What if we developed that choice into a fresh new habit? What if that new habit leads us to inner peace, a sense of purpose, loving relationships, and extraordinary energy? And what if by our example we taught our children, our business associates, and our friends to look for the WOO instead of the woe?

I promise that this is all not only possible but also simple, fulfilling, and fun. I've been living my life this way for the last thirty-five years, and I know beyond a doubt that WOOs are right there in front of me every day. I've laid the groundwork, muddled along through lots of trial and error, and emerged on the other side with a way that will make it easy for every one of us to enjoy every precious moment. The first step is to develop an eager spirit. I learned this lesson from one of the greatest teachers I have ever known.

I once asked John Wooden, "Coach, what's the difference between a good team and a great one?" The great basketball coach's answer took me by surprise. He said, "Brian, the difference between a good basketball team and a great one is the same difference between a good leader and a great one, a good parent and a great one, a good life and a great one. I believe the difference comes down to two little words. On good teams everyone is *willing* to support one another and the greater good. But great teams, teachers, parents, and leaders are *eager* to do whatever it takes. It's the difference between being willing and being eager that has the greatest impact on your performance, your character, and your impact on others."

Just as we all have hearts and minds, we have within us what I think of as an "eager meter." Picture a speedometer with *willing* at the zero mark and *eager* all the way at the other side, at 200 miles per hour. The most important truth about our eager meter is that we each are 100 percent in charge of our own, whether or not we think we have one. No one else controls our hope and faith in ourselves. No one else can ever give up for us. No one else can take us from good to great. We do that all by ourselves.

Why do some people seem to get all the breaks, caught in a perennial upward spiral? Is it merely luck or chance? Could it be that they live at a higher level on their eager meter?

I can always spot someone who has developed an eager spirit because their automatic, lighthearted response to most every WOO that comes their way is "The answer is *yes*. What's the question?"

Just as we can build a muscle, we can develop our sense of

eagerness. The most powerful, simple, and fun way to accelerate our eager meter is to begin to say yes to more WOOs, especially those that show up disguised as invitations that stretch
us beyond our comfort zones. As we elevate our ratio of yeses
to nos, we will find that we are choosing faith in ourselves over
fear of the unknown. A surefire way to hit the gas and shake
our future is by seeing the future through a lens of possibility.

One beautiful autumn evening, my friend Tom was relax-
ing on his patio thinking about his life after a long but satisfy-
ing day's work. He thought, *Wow! I am so lucky! I am living
a great life!* He had a beautiful home overlooking the ocean
in south Florida, and he had a great job. Best of all, he was in
love with a woman with whom he intended to spend the rest
of his life.

At the time, his focus outside of his own work was on his
fiancée's career. She was an up-and-coming singer, and Tom
was her manager. For two years he'd sacrificed every spare
moment to the project of landing a recording contract for
her. Earlier that afternoon he'd received the call they'd been
dreaming of day and night. A top record company was offering
her a lucrative deal. They would sign within a week! As he sat
there on the patio sipping an ice-cold beer, he thought things
just couldn't get any better.

A couple of days later he was dealt a blow he never saw coming. The woman he loved had found someone else. She wanted
Tom out of her life. Just like that, it was over. Her words hit him
like a freight train.

A year later he was living in a one-room apartment with
only his clothes, a futon mattress, and a television. The breakup
had hit him so hard that he just limped away, leaving her the
house and virtually all their other possessions. His life had
deteriorated rapidly into emptiness, his eager meter hovering

precariously close to zero. Listlessly he struggled to work each day, only to return to the tiny apartment and the silence that had become his only companion. Refusing to see friends or family, he had become a social hermit.

That New Year's Eve, as he sat alone in the darkness, he hit rock bottom. He realized he could no longer live this way. Either he was going to end it all or he would take back control of his life. As he teetered on the brink of suicide, a thought swept over him that would turn his life around. He decided then and there that he was going to make the next 365 days the "Year of the Tom."

He made a pledge to himself that every single day he would take at least one action that would enhance his life in some way—reading a book, watching a video, or listening to a recording that would help him in his career; spending quality time with a good friend; exercising; or attending a seminar or lecture on a subject in which he had interest. He had no idea where this would take him, but for the first time since the breakup it sparked hope and just the slightest flicker of eagerness.

He told his friends about the Year of the Tom and asked for their help. They had been so worried about Tom that they were thrilled to hear of his new sense of purpose. Several of them got together and brainstormed ways to help Tom. They came up with the inspired idea of forming the Intergalactic Annum Society—the official sponsors of the Year of the Tom. The society's charter was to "oversee the distribution of annual control" by keeping in constant touch with Tom. They even hosted a black-tie party where they awarded him a special certificate for bringing fresh meaning to his life through the Year of the Tom.

As the year progressed, Tom began to realize that many people go through life feeling helpless and without direction, just as he had when his girlfriend left him. They resign themselves to just getting by, wishing that something better would come along. This helplessness paralyzes them into believing they have no control over their lives and their happiness. They are barely willing to put one foot in front of the other, all eagerness and purpose drained away.

By creating his year of action and celebration, Tom accepted full responsibility for the quality of his life, and gradually empowered himself with the confidence to change it. He also looked at what had gone wrong, how he had overlooked many red flags that could have warned him in that relationship. He thought about the qualities he wanted in a woman with whom he could spend the rest of his life. This filled him not only with fresh hope but also with a resolve to never settle for less. Notch by notch, his eager meter began to rise.

By the end of the Year of the Tom, he had transformed his life in countless ways. He was engaged to a nurturing, intelligent woman who loved him unconditionally. He had been promoted to a management position and loved the new challenge and responsibility. He found he had enormous passion for mentoring and leading others. He had so much energy, he even started a side business in his spare time that generated substantial extra income and introduced him to many new friends. But the most dramatic change in his life was his newfound faith in possibility. He understood that not only do we have choices about what we do each day, but we also have the ultimate choice about the meaning we give to life's happenings. Tom's story is proof that even when it seems our lenses of possibility have been shattered, we have within us the special tools to put them back together.

In business, your eager meter has an enormous impact on the trajectory of your career. One of the most vivid examples of the results ignited by a truly eager spirit is the story of legendary director and producer Steven Spielberg. His pathway to one of the greatest careers in the movie industry is testimony to what is possible when you combine nearly off-the-charts eagerness with an unstoppable determination to seize the WOO.

From a very early age, Spielberg was enthralled with cinema. By the age of twelve he was already making what he called "adventure films," which were short 8 mm home movies. To earn his photography merit badge as a Boy Scout, he wrote and produced a short western he called *The Last Gunfight*. As he said years later when interviewed about his career, "That was how it all started." He was hooked on creating movies.

Though passionate and inspired about moviemaking, Spielberg was an unmotivated student in his regular classes. His eager meter was sparked only by his love of the movies. Through a family friend who was an executive at Universal Studios, seventeen-year-old Steven was given a short unpaid internship at the studio offices. However, this internship did not grant Steven admission to the movie lot where the films were being created. Undeterred by something as trivial as official access, and burning to learn everything he possibly could about film, Steven snuck onto the lot virtually every day. He pretended he belonged there and showed up in every department he could sneak into, watching, talking, and networking as if this was exactly what he was supposed to be doing. Though apprehended on several occasions and tossed off the lot, young Spielberg just kept coming back until he became so familiar to many of the crews that they accepted his presence as normal.

When it came to cinema, Spielberg, like the great white shark he would later make famous in *Jaws*, devoured absolutely everything he could clamp his jaws around. His passion and interest were so extraordinary that he simply couldn't get enough. He endeared himself to several crew members who were impressed by his unflagging enthusiasm.

Putting all of this hands-on learning to work, he produced and directed a short film called *Amblin'*. With that same irrepressible energy, driven by his eagerness, Steven kept pushing and pushing until he convinced Universal executives to take a look at his film. They were so blown away by the quality of his work that they signed Spielberg to a seven-year contract. He became the youngest director on contract at Universal Studios.

Forty-nine years later, the results of Spielberg's eager spirit are staggering. He has won three Academy Awards and his movies have generated over $10 billion worldwide. From *Jaws* to *Close Encounters of the Third Kind*, from *ET* to the Indiana Jones trilogy, from *Schindler's List* to *Saving Private Ryan*, Spielberg has touched hundreds of millions of lives through his stories, characters, and messages.

Some might look at his poor performance as a student growing up and characterize Steven Spielberg as an overachiever. Certainly none of his teachers saw in him someone who would become an American icon, a legend in the movie business. But Spielberg always had it in him to create a career that is a masterpiece, and the same is true of every one of us. There is more within you than others may have led you to believe. Spielberg's "genius" is less a result of DNA and more the outcome of his refusal to accept anything less than success, as measured by his eager meter. He transformed the WOOs he seized from an unofficial internship into an on-the-set education and eventually into an unparalleled career directing scores of movies adored the world over. You have the same WOO to create an amazing life.

A WOO for You

For the next week pay attention to how often you choose yes instead of no responses to experiences, challenges, and WOOs that may cause you to stretch beyond your comfort zones. Look for the yeses and nos that may be limiting you from traveling down the path you envision for yourself. What would happen to your spirit and your eager meter if you chose yes more often? How can you use no to your advantage, as a way to avoid bad or disruptive situations?

Look into your past and examine all your no or yes choices and how they contributed to who you are today. Have your yeses and nos taken you to the place you want to be? If not, how would you change those choices today? And how would you add to the choices you made in the past?

How can you elevate your eager meter from where it is now? Maybe it's time for the Year of You! Like you'd do with a great Spielberg film, enjoy the adventure!

2

What You Focus On Is What You Create

A seven-year-old boy stands atop a glistening, snow-covered hill, bursting with excitement as he prepares to zoom down the slope on his brand-new sled. The hillside is at least fifty yards wide and nearly perfect for a great run. There is only one obstacle in sight, a single stump about halfway down the hill, but there's lots of open hillside on either side of it. Just as he is about to kick off, he hears a well-meaning voice cry out, "Watch out for the stump!"

Whoosh—he's off. He rockets down the hill faster and faster, the icy wind whipping his red cheeks.

As he steers the sled that voice keeps repeating in his mind: *Watch out for the stump.* Swerving left and right as he picks up more and more speed, he can't seem to get that stump out of his thoughts. Then, *wham!* He crashes into the stump like a guided missile locked in on its target.

In fact, that little boy was programmed to crash into that stump. I know because I was that little boy. My sled was demolished, and though I sustained only a few bumps and bruises, my dignity was shattered. For a while after the incident, I was humiliated; I had crashed and burned. But ultimately my sledding ineptitude led me to an epiphany, a WOO from which I learned. We are taught—in fact, programmed—to be almost magnetically attracted to obstacles and fears, just as I was drawn to that stump. If we can change our focus, we can change our lives.

For years one of the cornerstones of personal growth has been "What we focus on is what we get." There is some truth in the statement, of course, but I've always felt it misses the essential ingredient that gives our focus power: ourselves. Isn't the more empowering truth that what we focus on is what we *create*? Our vision and focus unlatch the locks on those exciting windows of opportunity, but it's only through our energized and enthusiastic *actions* that we throw open those WOOs and improve our lives, relationships, health, and finances. Our vision creates *opportunities*. But it is our choices and actions that create our *results*.

We've all heard the saying "Luck happens to the prepared person." By having a vision about our future, we'll see opportunity in an entirely different way than others might. What may seem like a "lucky break" to those who lack our vision is, in fact, a purposeful choice.

A woman who attended one of my seminars recently had to make her way around the venue in a special wheelchair. Her spine had been damaged and her legs had been amputated after a terrible auto accident years before. In the seminar I led the participants through all kinds of physical exercises to teach key messages. She found ways to do every single one. As we prepared to break wooden boards karate style, as a metaphor for breaking through our fears and obstacles, she rolled her chair up to me and said with absolute conviction, "I am breaking the board!"

I was amazed at her determination. But I immediately thought, *How?* She must have read my mind, because she said, "I've been thinking about this all day since you said we get to do it. If you will put my board between two chairs and lift me from my chair so I can hit downward at it, I can do it!"

So I did.

With three hundred people cheering their lungs out, she tried at least ten times. But the board didn't break. Then, on the eleventh try, she broke through. When you're committed to something, you'll never quit after a mere ten attempts!

This remarkable young woman was committed to living her life fully. She recognized that she could choose where to apply her focus, and she understood that it gave her complete control over how she lived. Instead of fretting about what she couldn't do, she focused on what she *could* do. She focused on the WOOs rather than the obstacles. After she broke through that day, the other participants, deeply affected by her commitment, elevated their own commitment to break through and focus on possibility, not limitation.

As we begin to shift our focus more consistently away from the tree stumps in our path, to what we want rather than what we don't want, we live with greater passion. But passion is not stagnant and unchanging. Just as plants will die when they are not watered, not protected from the frost, or not repotted when they no longer fit into their surroundings, our passions require awareness, nurturing, and sometimes fresh action if they are to grow and flourish. When our passions change, it's time to adjust our focus.

Throughout my professional life, when my passion for my previous careers began to fade because of circumstances related to those positions, I made the decision to change my focus, to seek fresh new ways to ignite my passion. Though I loved being a swimming coach and owned and operated CLASS Aquatics, one of the largest and most successful swimming programs in the country, I felt the need to change because I had no balance in my life. My work in those years was *everything*—it was all-consuming. When I realized that I knew myself only as a coach, that I had no life away from the pool deck, I recognized that I wanted to change. I had created a tremendously successful professional life, but with absolutely no balance. It was time to create a new focus on a life with passion both at work *and* at home.

So I left coaching and enrolled in graduate school at UCLA. I had virtually no money. But I knew that for *things* to change, *I* must change. And that change begins with new focus. A dear friend helped me with a loan that, combined with the income I received from the sale of CLASS Aquatics, made it possible for me to finance my two years at UCLA. So I seized the WOO and jumped into graduate school with passion. Instead of focusing on the risk of the leap I was taking and what could go wrong, I was hungry to learn, excited to connect with my classmates, and thrilled with this completely new adventure. My focus was determinedly on what could go *right*.

And I had an absolute blast at UCLA. Once again, it was my passion for people that made the difference. I became the president of the Graduate School of Management Student Association and with a team of brilliant and talented students tackled any number of challenging projects, including fun and effective ways to improve the association's finances and put them into the black for the first time in a decade. That seemed in keeping with what we learned in business school.

At graduation I was given the Dean's Award for Outstanding Service. In past years the president of the Student Association was ineligible for this award. But the students and faculty who were responsible for choosing the recipient decided to change the eligibility rule because they felt my contributions were so extraordinary. I was stunned and deeply moved. When we are honored for simply giving, without any thought or expectation of getting something in return, it is the most meaningful and fulfilling experience imaginable.

While at UCLA I began my search for balance. I started running every day and found that I absolutely loved it. I became far fitter than I had ever been in my life. But the spiritual joy and inspiration I found in running dwarfed even the considerable physical benefits. The more I ran, the clearer it was to me that I had never really taken time to be present in the moment with myself before. Running became a blissful quiet time of reflection, percolation, peace, and presence. I never consciously tried to figure things out when I ran, but without fail, creative ideas and solutions to challenges that had me completely stumped would emerge like magic.

The most important part of my new focus on balance had to do with relationships. During my years as a coach I hid my fear of relationships behind my fanatical focus on work. By immersing myself so completely in my swimmers and the development of the team, I created the perfect comfort zone. But that comfort zone was actually a solitary confinement zone. I didn't really know who I *was*—I only knew what I *did*. At UCLA I began to understand that no one can be loved until he lets himself be seen. No one can be seen until he learns to love himself. As I began to develop balance physically, emotionally, mentally, and spiritually for the first time in my life, I began to like the person I was becoming.

The combination of newly found balance with my passion

for what I was doing opened my eyes, swept away my fears of inadequacy, and brought me the greatest gift of my life—meeting my future wife. In a moment of serendipity we found each other on a one-day business trip I made to Anchorage, Alaska, during my summer internship while at UCLA. Here is how I wrote about the magic between us in our wedding book:

> Before I knew you I wondered where you were. I searched for you everywhere, hoping to find you in everyone I met. I couldn't find you. I began to wonder if you truly existed. Once, long ago, I wrote down a thought that could have shown me the way to you—if only I would have listened to my own words. *No one can be loved until they let themselves be seen—no one can be seen until they learn to love themselves.* Two years ago I set out to find myself. When I finally began to like the person I had become, to truly accept myself, I began to think, to smile, and to talk. I stopped looking for you when I found myself—and there you were.

And so the third and most precious of all my passions took root in my heart: my love for my wife and daughters, a love that means everything to me.

It is the interweaving of these three passions—family and friends I adore, work I treasure, and daily movement and exercise to fuel my energy—that make me feel like I am the luckiest man on the face of the earth.

The key lesson I learned from this meandering path is that passion doesn't always just show up. I had to look for it, be open to it, and, most of all, boldly grasp it when it came within reach. I had to stop focusing on the stumps and start flying down the slope with abandon. When you think about it, don't we all have a choice to live with passion or to merely settle? And that choice is more important than talent.

One of my daughters' dance teammates became a perfect example of passion trumping innate talent. Lindsey was at best a fair dancer through her high school years. She didn't possess the natural talent and balance as a dancer that was so apparent in a few of the girls. She was never chosen for the leading roles in the dance studio's productions. But Lindsey *loved* dancing, loved it with a passion. While others faded away from dance in their college years, Lindsey seized every WOO she could find to dance and perform. She graduated with a degree in dance and has been performing at Walt Disney World for almost a decade. She lives with joy because she found her passion and immersed herself in it every day. She focused on what she wanted and never stopped until she had created it.

My friend John Wooden often said, "There are no over-achievers. We are all underachievers." When we focus on our passions and seize every WOO that leads us in the direction of those passions, like Lindsey, we will come closer to our true potential far more consistently. For what we focus on is what we create.

A WOO for You

Now it's your turn for some tree stump removal.

1. For ten or fifteen minutes, make a list of the things that aren't working in your life the way you would like. This shouldn't take long because we know what is keeping us from feeling passionate. These are your tree stumps.

2. Now let's focus on the glistening WOOs that abound around us. For the next week, start your day by:

a. Appreciating what you've already accomplished and listing at least three achievements—however minor they may seem—each day.

b. Thinking of the people closest to you and finding one new positive trait you hadn't noticed before about them. Take a moment to truly admire that quality. Are there ways you might model it yourself?

c. Thinking of your work and considering what might happen if you did a little reprogramming by creating some simple, fresh actions to prepare for your day. Think of the possibilities! You could lay your clothes out the night before. Or for a week you could set your alarm so that you wake up ten minutes earlier than the previous day, and in a week you'll have an extra hour just for you. You can use this time to exercise, meditate, sing in the shower, write in a journal, write personal cards or letters, prepare something light and healthy for breakfast, or say thoughtful goodbyes as you look into the faces of your loved ones and tell them you hope they have a splendid day and that you can't wait to hear every detail at dinner that night.

This new morning practice just might start you in a whole new direction. What if you arrived at work feeling great about who you are, relaxed, confident, and ready to seize the day?

Remember, we've never been taught to start our day by consistently focusing on and being ready to look for and embrace the WOOs. Once we do, how much easier would it be for our battered or depleted passions to be renewed once again? Maybe we'd remember what we enjoy: playing music . . . dancing in the kitchen . . . smiling for no particular reason.

It doesn't take that much to find authentic inner peace. You may find that this simple method is transformational and positively affects everything you do and every person with whom you come in contact.

3

The Past Does Not Equal the Future

It is truly freeing when we recognize that our past does not have to define our future unless it serves us. In other words, we can change in an instant. And when we do change it will not only affect our own direction and performance; it can have a powerful impact on others through our example of transformation.

I have completed four marathons in my life and have great respect for the training, preparation, and effort it takes to run twenty-six miles. When I finished my first marathon my spirit was on top of the world. But my legs were at the bottom. They wanted to go on an immediate sit-down strike. I could barely convince them to carry me to my car. I was proud of what I'd achieved, in part because I felt like I had reached the limit of what my body was capable of handling.

So when I learned that there are several races around the world each year called ultra-marathons, I was in awe. An ultra is any race longer than a marathon. For example, each year in the foothills of the Sierras in California they run the Western States 100—a 100-mile race. But the king of the ultras has been run in Australia from Sydney to Melbourne for more than thirty years. The distance of this absurdly challenging race is 875 kilometers, or 544 miles.

In 1983 a man named Cliff Young showed up to run this race. No one in the elite ultra-marathon-running community had ever seen Cliff before, and two things stuck out about him as soon as they saw him. First, he looked a bit older than the other runners. And second, he wasn't dressed like the other elite runners. He didn't have the up-to-date running shoes and shorts everyone else in the field was wearing. He certainly didn't have a sponsor.

When they asked Cliff what his racing experience was, he answered quite unabashedly, "I've never run a race before in my life. But I've lived on a sheep station for most of my years and have never had a horse to chase the sheep. So I thought to myself, why not give her a go?"

As he warmed up, some people actually started laughing. His form was nothing like that of the other runners. In fact the best description of Cliff's style was that he ran like a wet noodle. His arms hung limply by his sides and he shuffled along, barely lifting his feet off the ground. Most of those watching thought there was no way he'd make it five miles, much less five hundred. Instead of measuring him as competition, they likely thought, *Get the paramedics.*

When it came to effectively running this race, past knowledge and experience had taught that the only way to do it was to run no more than twelve to fifteen hours in each twenty-four-hour period. All of the elite ultra-athletes ran the race this way, believing that if you didn't rest and recuperate long enough each day, you would break down and be unable to complete the distance.

But no one had ever told Cliff that. And no one had ever told the sheep that "trained" him. If Cliff had decided to rest for four hours when chasing sheep on his station, they would be gone.

So with this rather unique ovine training and experience guiding him, Cliff ran the first twenty-four hours without a break. He simply didn't know that the past experience and knowledge of the top experts in the field of ultra-marathoning taught that this was an enormous mistake. He just kept noodling along, chasing invisible sheep.

Not only did Cliff win the race that year, but he broke the previous record by nearly two days.

As amazing as his performance was, it wasn't the most remarkable element of the story. Guess what happened the next year? Four different people broke Cliff's record. How did they do it? They noodled. Cliff had rendered the past expertise about ultra-marathoning obsolete through his completely unexpected performance and strategy. It turned out that this funny-looking running style was the most efficient way to run such an ultra-long distance. These runners adapted to this unusual style and broke a record that would have seemed superhuman before Cliff's performance. Cliff helped them see that the past does not equal the future.

And that's still not the best part of the story. You see, when Cliff broke this world record he was sixty-one years old. How many of us give up on ourselves because we are too old, too young, too this, or too that? Just as we've been taught to look out for the obstacles instead of the WOOs, most of us have been programmed to believe that the past *does* equal the future. We affirm to ourselves, "I've never been able to lose that weight . . . guess I never will." "I've always been afraid of public speaking . . . always will be." "I've never kept up a regular exercise program . . . guess I just don't have what it takes." As John Wooden taught me, there are no overachievers. We all have more in us than we think. Only when we truly believe that the past does not have to define the future can we open ourselves to new and brighter possibilities.

When we develop the belief within us, we open ourselves to discovering and seizing more WOOs. Howard Schultz, the visionary behind Starbucks and its chairman and CEO, is a shining example of this powerful truth. When I interviewed Howard on my national radio show he said his belief that the past does not have to equal the future is at the very core of his company's unprecedented success and social impact.

Starbucks is in many ways the quintessential people-focused company. Schultz's vision for Starbucks from the beginning was an establishment with a special relationship with its customers, providing what he called a "third place" for them—a place of comfort between work and home centered around a high-quality coffee experience. At that time there was absolutely nothing like this.

Schultz believed that in order to exceed the expectations of customers his company had to first exceed the expectations of its own people.

Schultz grew up in federally subsidized housing with parents who faced many health issues. His father never earned more than $20,000 a year and the family was often without health insurance. To Howard these struggles came to represent the fracturing of the American dream. He was determined that this past would not define the future for him or the people he could affect.

So when he began to build Starbucks in the mid-1980s he saw a WOO to create a new kind of company that would balance the importance of profitability with a social conscience, based upon a very different relationship with employees. Though by the end of 1987 Starbucks consisted of only eleven stores and a total of about one hundred employees, Howard refused to accept that the past had to equal the future and established two cornerstones that transformed his company.

First, all employees, including the 60 percent who worked part-time, would always receive comprehensive health insurance. Second, all employees would have the chance to own part of their company through stock options. This led to employees being renamed "partners" and to a company that has become a cultural icon and one of the great success stories in American business history. Today Starbucks employs nearly two hundred thousand partners worldwide in more than twenty-one thousand stores.

From this day forward, as we sip our latte or caramel Frappuccino, why not let it serve as a delicious reminder that the past does not equal the future? Ignited by this powerful belief, we just may discover WOOs that can lead us to our own personal success stories.

A WOO for You

What might you discover if you identified those areas of your life where you are holding yourself back because you are acting as if the past *does* equal the future? Why not focus especially on areas in which you truly want to break through? Here are a few examples to help you get started:

- Overcoming your fear of public speaking.
- Becoming more organized.
- Sticking to a regular exercise program.
- Losing that weight.
- Arriving ten minutes early to every appointment instead of late.

- Becoming debt-free over the next twelve months or twenty-four months. (You can set the schedule according to your level of debt. If you have substantial school loans, that period might be ten years. But, my friend, it is doable.)

Once you've identified your breakthrough targets, prepare a simple game plan for the next thirty days where you decide to take specific action at least three times each week in that new direction. Celebrate your small victories as they come up. In just thirty days you will have taken a minimum of twelve steps away from a past that didn't serve you, toward your new future. Inch by inch, anything's a cinch.

STAGE TWO

ENERGIZE AND ENGAGE

4

A New Kind of Energy— Going from 3 to 10!

What is the ultimate secret to a life of fulfillment? I've been fascinated by this question my entire life. After decades of working with people to develop their performance, zest for life, and inner peace, it is clear to me that the ultimate secret is our *energy*. The challenge is that almost everyone I know thinks that their energy level is something that happens to them rather than something they create. Our energy is not like the weather; it is a matter of our choice. When we decide that our energy level is our choice—and, even more important, how to create a consistently better energy choice—we hold the key to make our life better. And the rule of the game for a life of extraordinary energy is simply to *play full out*.

What are the foundational reasons our energy is so vital? The first is simply that energy helps us seize more WOOs. Isn't it amazing that when we have more energy, obstacles don't seem so tough, challenges so immense? Napoleon Hill wrote in his timeless classic *Think and Grow Rich*, "Within every adversity is planted the seed of equivalent or greater benefit."

When we fill with energy, we shift immediately to the potential benefit. Without energy, all we see is the adversity.

The second reason that energy is so important is that it is the secret to igniting and inspiring others as well as ourselves. Don't we all want to ignite and inspire someone, whether it is our loved ones, our teammates, our employees, or ourselves? The instant we recognize that, to everyone we care about, our energy *is* our example, our life changes. People will remember very little of what we say, no matter how well we say it. But they'll never forget our energy. They get our energy long before we open our mouths and long after we close them. They get our energy over the phone although they've never seen our face. They even get our energy in the way we send emails. To me, the word *email* doesn't stand for "electronic mail"; it stands for "energy mail."

The third reason energy is so important is particularly crucial in business today. Every client for whom I speak, regardless of the industry, is deeply concerned about how to deal better with change and generate breakthrough results. When we consider that less than a decade ago a tweet was a sound birds made, 5G was a parking place, Skype was a typo, and LinkedIn was a prison, it's clear to see that technology certainly is a driving force behind the acceleration of change. Within many organizations a new functional area has been established called change management. But true champions of change are far more focused on change leadership than on change management. Whereas change management is about making small, incremental adjustments one at a time, or implementing change in a series of manageable steps, change leadership seeks to initiate change on a much bigger scale. Change management tries to encourage people to adapt to change; change leadership is all about empowering people to create positive change.

Change management is reactive. Change leadership is proactive. And the secret to proactivity is energy and engagement.

The venerable Gallup organization, the leader in statistical polling, publishes an annual report called *State of the American Workplace*. The report provides statistical evidence that employee engagement is strongly correlated to job performance factors such as turnover, absenteeism, safety, productivity, and profitability. For example, retail technology giant Best Buy was able to connect employee engagement scores to store performance and found that for every one-tenth of a point increase in employee engagement, the store saw a $100,000 increase in operating income.

According to the Gallup report, just 29 percent of employees across all industries in the United States and Canada consider themselves to be fully engaged in their work. Yet these 29 percent are the teammates we love to work beside. When faced with challenge and immense change, their mantra is "Oh yeah!" The study goes on to report that a whopping 54 percent say they are disengaged, and an even more disconcerting 18 percent claim to be *actively* disengaged, indicating that they are unhappy and unproductive at work and liable to spread negativity to co-workers. The mantra for these disengaged employees is "Oh no!"

How do we turn these statistics around in our organization and boost employee engagement to extraordinary levels? How do we improve our own level of engagement? The key is energy.

How can we live each day with extraordinary energy? How can we create the *habit* of enhanced energy?

The simplest way I have found to build consistent energy is to think of it in relation to a 10-point scale. On that scale, 1 is comatose, while 10 is the energy level of a child arriving at

Disneyland for the first time, or the way we feel in those moments when we just know there's nothing we can't accomplish. The billion-dollar question to ask ourselves is, "On that scale from 1 to 10, where are we living our life now?" And if we're not yet living with the energy level we want, how do we change that?

There are two secrets to elevating our energy level on a consistent basis. The first offers the most immediate impact.

Our energy is created by the way we *move*. In other words, anytime we've been at our best, anytime we've been most creative, most confident, and most alive, we have moved distinctly differently than when we've not been at our best. When we change our posture, facial expression, eye position, and breathing, we instantly change our energy. When we change our energy, we change our life.

I've said this to some individuals and groups before, and they reply, "Brian, if I had more energy, I'd move more." To which I love to reply, "Ah, but if you move more, you'll have more energy." The horse comes before the cart—our movement generates our horsepower.

If you don't believe me, try this right now. Straighten your spine and sit or stand up tall. Lift your chin and put a huge, goofy grin on your face. Open your eyes wide and take a wonderful, deep breath. Do you feel an immediate rise in your energy meter? In fact, it's impossible to feel sad or down when your body is elevated in this way. It is no coincidence that some of our best ideas seem to pop into our heads when we're taking a shower. It's all that movement that ignites our creativity.

To change our movement habits so that we ignite a consistently higher energy level, we may need to apply something that I call the *principle of exaggeration*. When I was a swimming coach, many of the kids struggled with a common technique flaw in the freestyle stroke. They were stuck in the habit of not pulling their stroke far enough under the center of their body, the spot where they had the greatest leverage and power. But if I attempted to correct swimmers who had developed a wide arm pull by saying, "Pull down the centerline of your body," what do you think they said to me in response? They'd look at me as if I had lost my marbles, and reply in exasperation, "I am." Isn't that exactly the same response we hear inside our own head when we seek to make positive changes that shake us out of our comfort zones? So when I was a coach, it was crucial for me to remember that what I saw did not match what my swimmers were feeling. They thought they were already swimming correctly. These kids had become comfortable pulling wide under their bodies. The feeling was ingrained in them as a habit.

So it did absolutely no good to tell them how to do it. I had to apply the principle of exaggeration. I instructed them to pull as far across their body underwater as they could, so that the right hand swept way left under their bodies and the left hand crossed way over to the right. As soon as they attempted to follow these instructions, guess where they pulled? Like magic, their pull came right down under the centerline of the body.

As they exaggerated in this way, how do you think it felt? At first it was strange. But the more they stayed with it, the more natural the motion became. Soon they settled into the new habit.

Like with my swimmers, our current patterns of movement are nothing more than habits. And by applying the principle of exaggeration, we can change lethargy into vitality and elevate ourselves sharply on the energy scale. We can use this principle to invigorate ourselves by moving our bodies more actively, just as the swimmers used the principle to improve their strokes. As strange as it will feel at first to sit up taller, to smile more, to add bounce to our steps and spark to our spirits, in a very short time it will feel even stranger to go back to our previous patterns.

When we recognize that our energy is created by the way that we move, and when we embrace the responsibility to elevate our energy, we not only position ourselves to seize more WOOs, we actually create them. To everyone we touch, our energy is our example. It's our calling card, our brand, our invitation. In even seemingly mundane everyday interactions, our energy can make a remarkable difference in the impact we have on others personally and professionally.

I had been given my least favorite task on my long honey-do list: returning items my wife had decided she didn't want after all. As I stood in a long line at TJ Maxx waiting to return the items, I passed the time observing the seven or eight customer service associates working the registers. It was the very end of the retail day, and both customers and associates looked weary and ready to complete their transactions and head home.

After a moment or two I found myself drawn to a young, tall, and athletic-looking associate. It was her kind smile and easy warmth with each customer she served that attracted my attention. I noticed that when her customers gathered their bags and left her register they seemed a little lighter, with a little more spring in their step than the other shoppers. That welcoming energy she inspired made me hope that I would end up at her register.

As luck would have it, that's just what happened. And sure enough, she greeted me as if I was the most important person on the planet. I couldn't help but feel she was genuinely happy to see me, though we had never met before. And so I immediately seized the WOO.

Returning her radiant smile, I said, "You know, I've noticed as I waited in line how you seem to make every person who comes to your register happy and appreciated. I was hoping I'd end up with you taking care of my return because I wanted to tell you what a wonderful representative you are for TJ Maxx. You really make a difference with your warmth, generosity, and kindness."

Completely taken aback by my praise, she said, almost blushing, "You made my day!" Her surprise at my praise made it clear that she didn't provide this delightful service to win praise or credit. She did it because she cared about lifting others' spirits. Her authenticity sprang from her desire to give, not to get.

As she worked through my return she told me the story of where she came by her inspiration. "When I was a little girl we often stopped by Krispy Kreme on the way to school. We were almost always taken care of by the kindest lady I've ever met. She was sweeter than the doughnuts! I told my mom that when I grew up I wanted to be just like my Krispy Kreme hero because she always made everyone feel so happy. I think of her almost every day when I come to work."

As I prepared to leave I thanked her again for the joy she gave me and others. I told her that her story made me think of my favorite movie, the Christmas classic *It's a Wonderful Life*. In the Frank Capra masterpiece, a hardworking, seemingly average guy named George Bailey (played by Jimmy Stewart) sees himself as a failure, a man who failed to pursue his dreams or achieve his goals. He is blind to the enormous difference he has made in the lives of so many through his daily kindnesses, his countless thoughtful actions in service to others, and the unshakable loyalty he demonstrates to his family, friends, and community. It took his guardian angel, Clarence, to awaken George to the tremendous positive impact he had made, and to the fact that he truly lived a wonderful life. I wanted to be sure this wonderful young woman recognized that, like her Krispy Kreme role model and like George Bailey, she made this world a better and brighter place each day.

It is vital that you recognize, that you accept, that you know that you are already important. You are already significant. The WOO is already there for you in your every interaction, and in every seemingly average day. As Mother Teresa said, "It's not what we do that makes the difference. It's the love we put into the doing." Each act of kindness, thoughtfulness, unselfish giving, and warmth not only elevates those around you but ignites them to do the same. And so, like the Olympic flame, the light is handed from carrier to carrier until it circles the world. Seize that next window of opportunity. It may be the most important one of all!

The second secret to living with higher energy is to focus more consistently on our purpose. When we think of anyone we admire, whether it's someone we know personally or someone about whom we've studied or read, it is crystal clear that they are living purposefully.

One of the greatest books I've ever read is *Man's Search for Meaning* by Viktor Frankl. He was one of the most famous psychiatrists of the twentieth century; the book details his experience during the years he spent imprisoned in a concentration camp in Nazi Germany. The most powerful insight I gained from this remarkable book had to do with purpose. Frankl explained that if anyone had tried to predict which prisoners would survive the Holocaust on the basis of their physical health and strength before imprisonment, they would have failed. The ultimate determinant of life or death for these battered and starving human beings was not physical stamina but rather a purpose, something they felt they had left undone but needed to finish. Whether it was a child they had to return to, work they felt they alone could complete, or a cause they had to serve, it was *purpose* that gave them the strength to take their next breath.

By bringing elevated movement and greater focus to our sense of purpose in our daily life, we will begin to experience a rise on the ten-point energy scale. As we move from 6.5 to 7.4 to 8.3 to 9.1, everything that matters to us in life will move in that same positive direction. We will live with extraordinary energy. Professionally we will see our engagement level soar as we move from "Oh no!" to "Oh yeah!" As leaders, we can apply this same simple but powerful metric to our team, asking ourselves, "Where are we as an organization on that 10-point scale?" With this new energy habit we will place ourselves in the best possible position to seize more WOOs.

A WOO for You

In the next chapter I'll suggest some powerful questions to help you find your purpose. But here is a simple first step. What if you asked yourself every morning when you awaken, and every night right before you go to bed, "What am I truly grateful about in my life?" then allow yourself to fully feel that appreciation? Focusing on what you're grateful for could guide you to your priorities. And you might discover that your priorities are the pathway to your purpose.

5

Expired or Inspired?

Is there one absolutely crucial ingredient that enables us to reach our full potential? After a lifetime of working with people in three different careers—as a high-performance athletic coach and business owner, as a corporate executive, and as a professional speaker—it is crystal clear to me that one ingredient is essential. That vital ingredient is *inspiration*. Without it we will never approach all we can be.

I bring a laminated photo of my wife and daughters to every event at which I speak. The very last thing I do before beginning my presentation is to focus on that picture and spend a moment of connection with each of my girls as I look into their faces. Then I touch my heart and dedicate my presentation to them. It may be corny, but instantly it changes me. I become energized and inspired. No matter how many days I've been on the road, no matter how many airport delays I've encountered or how much sleep I've missed, none of it matters. I am on fire because of the purpose with which my wife and daughters fill me. As I look out into the audience I see Carole, Kelsey, and Jenna and believe with all my heart that if I don't give the participants everything I've got, I'm not giving my girls everything I've got.

What is the greatest source of our inspiration and energy? After years of coaching elite athletes, working with and interviewing some of the most accomplished and influential leaders in business, education, and healthcare, speaking around the world to some of the most successful organizations on the planet, and perhaps most revealing, having poured my heart and soul into trying to be the best father and husband I can be, it is clear to me that the ultimate source of inspiration is our purpose. It can move us beyond adversity and obstacles to enthusiasm, peak performance, and passion. In a very real sense, if we're not inspired, we're on our way to being expired.

So how do we find our purpose? There may be the rare person who knows their purpose from an early age, but for most of us it's not so simple. Most often our pathway to purpose is a journey with many twists and turns. Some of those forays may even appear to be dead ends. But the secret to navigating this journey to purpose is to pay attention and seize the WOOs as we encounter them along the way.

The one to four hours I have with clients as I deliver my talks are precious WOOs because I am living my purpose—to help everyone I touch break through fears, obstacles, habits, and doubts that keep them from being who they truly are. I've discovered my purpose in the same way each of us must: by *asking* and *acting*. Because our purpose is already inside us, it is a matter of digging it out like buried treasure. But it's vital to remember that this is buried treasure we know is there. Our absolute faith that we can discover our purpose is the essential starting place for our treasure hunt. Steve Jobs, in a Stanford commencement address, said, "You can't connect the dots looking forward; you can only connect them looking backward. So you have to trust that the dots will somehow connect in your future." When we find our purpose and then act upon it consistently, we open windows of opportunity we would otherwise have missed.

Here are some questions to help us mine deep in our heart to uncover our inspiring purpose:

1. What would you do if you knew you couldn't fail?

2. What makes you completely lose track of time and forget to eat, and causes all your aches, pains, and discomfort to magically disappear?

3. For what do you want to be remembered?

4. What did your eight-year-old self dream of?

5. What have been your greatest successes and biggest failures in your life?

6. What brings you the greatest joy and makes you feel the most alive?

7. What are you best at? What are your true strengths?

8. What do you have an insatiable desire to learn more about?

9. What really catches your attention and ignites your emotion?

10. In your past, what has grabbed your heart and brought you to tears of elation, inspiration, and passion?

When we ask these questions of ourselves, clear patterns emerge and solidify. Then comes the fun part. We can now take action in the direction of our answers and open our eyes to WOOs that are in alignment with our purpose. As Christopher Reeve put it, "So many of our dreams at first seem impossible, then they seem improbable, and then, when we summon the will, they soon become inevitable."

When you meet Prosper Nwankpa, you immediately sense his warmth and calming presence. His smile is so easy, unforced, and authentic that you can't help but feel a little lighter no matter what may be on your mind. I've rarely ever met a person who brings such a feeling of peace and perspective to others without saying a word, conveying an absolute faith that all will be well.

He is so humble and unassuming you'd have no idea that though he is only in his early thirties, Prosper has already created, built, and sold two multimillion-dollar software companies, though he never even touched a computer until he was nearly twenty years old. Prosper's is a story of seizing the WOO, of unstoppable purpose and inspiration, and ultimately of *sharing* the WOO. He has taught me that the greatest of all WOOs are those we open for others, the WOOs we pay forward.

Prosper grew up one of five children in Aba, a city in the West African country of Nigeria. He was raised in a deeply spiritual family whose foundation was firmly rooted in the religious beliefs and practices of their village. His family was poor, with barely enough to eke out a simple life. He attended public school because the private boarding school in his hometown was far too costly to even consider. The public schools were extremely run down, with dirt floors and ancient, broken-down furniture and equipment. Though Prosper showed real promise in school and loved to learn, it seemed that his path in life was predestined to poverty and the continuation of his own family's meager existence.

There was one light that shined on the outskirts of young Prosper's universe—his uncle who lived in America. He was almost a mythical figure to Prosper because he had immigrated to the United States to receive a better education than he could have found in Nigeria, and had gone on to earn a successful living in his new country.

This uncle was the first to awaken Prosper to the power of opportunity when he decided to pay for Prosper to attend boarding school. The annual cost, $1,500, was so far out of Prosper's reach that it seemed nearly inconceivable that anyone could offer such a gift. Prosper was so deeply inspired by his uncle's generosity that he became utterly determined to excel beyond anyone's expectations, so that he could somehow repay his extraordinary kindness.

He left home at age eleven to attend this school; the early separation from his family was just one of the sacrifices he had to make on his journey toward success. Despite the difficult conditions at his new school—studying by the light from a kerosene lantern at night, limited food rations, the harsh discipline of corporal punishment and waking up at 5:00 a.m. to start the daily routines of boarding school life—young Prosper learned responsibility, self-reliance, and determination to excel. He showed exceptional promise in his studies and his grades soared. But the harsh reality was that the private school, though better in quality than the public school, still had a weak curriculum that would not prepare him to be competitive in the larger world.

His uncle planted the idea that if Prosper was to have a real opportunity, he must consider leaving Nigeria to study in America. His parents were saddened to be losing their son at such a young age, but they made peace with the fact that opportunities like this come once in a lifetime, and so they supported the move. At fifteen, the agony of separation from his family weighing on his heart, he left Nigeria for New York and enrolled in Columbus High School, a public high school in the Bronx.

New York was quite a shock for the young man, who had never been outside his village before. In the first year or two of his time there he was belittled by most of the other kids for being different. He dressed very simply, grateful to have shoes and completely ignorant of and uninterested in the name on the label. He was shocked by the way the other students treated their teachers. In his previous school in Nigeria, teachers received great respect and were always addressed politely.

When Prosper demonstrated this same level of respect to his teachers in the Bronx, his classmates thought he was kissing up to them. It took almost two years of continuing his consistent respectful attitude before he was accepted for who he was.

During his junior year, a recruiter named Phil Smith from Williams College visited his high school looking for minority students with potential. Prosper was one of two students accepted into Williams that year and given a full scholarship. Tuition at the time was $50,000 a year. More and more light was streaming into Prosper's life through the window his uncle had opened for him. Each ray of new possibility fired within Prosper a stronger drive to honor his uncle's faith and family's support and sacrifice.

When Nigerian children immigrate to America, the hopes and dreams of their families are directed toward one occupation—becoming a doctor. It is the ultimate demonstration of success, the only truly acceptable validation of one's education. Prosper's family felt the same way and expected nothing less.

During his first year at Williams, Prosper followed this well-worn path, concentrating his studies on pre-med. Though he did very well in his courses, he did not feel a burning passion to become a physician. In his sophomore year he decided to enroll in a computer science class. It was his very first experience with a computer. It was like learning an entirely new language.

He failed miserably. He started the class so far behind his classmates in terms of experience and familiarity with computers that he simply couldn't catch up in a single semester. There were only two black students in the course; the other, also an African immigrant, struggled just as much as Prosper and ended up dropping out of the class. But despite his ineptitude, Prosper found the field fascinating and genuinely fun. It fired his interest far more than any of his pre-med courses. His teacher awarded him a C+ more because of his attitude and effort than his performance, and in the almost certain belief Prosper would not continue with other computer science classes.

But she underestimated the depth of Prosper's inspiration. Not only did he immediately enroll in more computer science courses, he immersed himself in the world of computers and software. He seized every WOO, showing up at office hours to ask questions and receive individual support. He studied and worked harder than he ever had before. A year later he enrolled in a robotics course taught by the same professor who had generously given him that C+ in his first computer science class. She could hardly believe he was the same student.

A boy raised to believe he was destined to live in poverty in a small city in Nigeria, he had now graduated with honors from one of the finest academic institutions in America. Prosper had grown to believe that possibility was ever-present for those who looked for it. So, together with two classmates, he decided to start a company rather than look for a job.

Starting the company meant lots of sleepless nights. Once he spent seventy-two straight hours with no sleep, coding to meet a deadline. It was at this point that he received a call from a potential investor, someone who would turn out to be one of the largest investors in the budding company. Prosper was so sleep-deprived that he literally hung up on this potential investor. Luckily for Prosper, the man called back later, and ended up investing $300,000 in Prosper's start-up company.

Prosper went to Pakistan to live for eight months while he built the company in order to keep operating costs down. He ended up building a team there and worked hard to secure U.S. visas for most of the employees who showed promise. For him, it was important to give his employees a WOO like the one he had received.

Within three years they had attracted more than two million users worldwide to their social networking enterprise, called Xuqa, and Prosper had developed code for functions and features that had never been available on any other site. They achieved success internationally, and a Turkish company purchased Xuqa for several million dollars.

During his time building Xuqa, Prosper realized there was a burning need for online companies to find innovative ways to monetize their services beyond selling advertising. So his next venture was to develop a company that seized this WOO. Peanut Labs rapidly became a cutting-edge leader in online marketing research and monetization. They match online consumers and shoppers with companies seeking to engage them, discover what they want, and serve those needs. After three years of eighteen-hour days spent coding, creating, and refining nearly nonstop, Prosper and his partners sold Peanut Labs to E-Rewards, the largest data collection company in the world.

While Prosper was building these companies he never forgot his family and how difficult life remained back in Nigeria. He made it his purpose to help them in every way he could, and visited every chance he got. When his mother became very ill, she did her best to keep the severity of her illness hidden from Prosper so he would not worry. Shortly after he sold Peanut Labs his mother fell into a diabetic coma and Prosper was finally informed of what had been happening with her. Apprehensive about seeking help from healthcare professionals, she had turned to her religion for healing, praying for a miracle. Sad to say, she died before he saw her again.

His mother's passing had a profound effect on Prosper. He no longer wanted to build businesses simply to make money. Even though he was now giving back and helping pay for education for his cousins, nephews, and nieces, he wanted to earn those dollars by making a real difference in this world. He could not get out of his mind a belief that his mother's death had awakened in his spirit: *The stories we tell ourselves enough eventually become our autobiographies.* Prosper's new passion and purpose was to help as many people as he possibly could to create better stories for themselves that would lead them to triumph and freedom, rather than tragedy and fear.

Together with a friend from college, Daniel Jacobs, Prosper created the idea of a company built upon the power of stories. Their company is called AVANOO, which means "open to the now." Daniel and Prosper have partnered with around two hundred speakers and authors to create online video programs on leadership, thriving on change, communication, life balance, presentation skills, team building, purpose, sales, social media marketing, and many other areas of personal and professional development. Each eighteen-day program consists of two-to-three-minute videos that come directly to their clients' emails. AVANOO has worked with leaders in video-based learning research at the University of California at San Diego to develop the visual imagery for these videos and the format of story, message, and action in each short video. With programs in place for NBC, KPMG, Chico's, several municipal government teams, FujiFilm, Kaiser Permanente, and many more, AVANOO is reaching hundreds of thousands of individuals with empowering stories of possibility and opportunity.

From his determination to emulate his uncle by providing a better education for his family members to his commitment to help as many people as he possibly can to create stories of hope and inspiration for themselves, Prosper demonstrates the power of unstoppable inspiration every single day. It would be easy to say that, coming from an impoverished background, Prosper is an overachiever. But he would be the first to tell you that he considers himself an inspired human being who has so much more he wants to accomplish in this world. Every day he wants to become a better father, husband, uncle, innovator, coder, leader, and human being. And he knows that is possible because we have more gifts within us than we can imagine. It is inspiration, supported by perspiration and imagination, that propels us to the destination of our greatest dreams.

The power of developing and instilling and inspiring purpose within an organization has the same kind of transformative impact upon collective energy as it does on an individual. I have had the privilege to speak more than twenty-five times over the years for nurses, physicians, administrative employees, and executives at Kaiser Permanente. This healthcare giant is an HMO (health maintenance organization) with nearly 10 million members. Kaiser Permanente is the only health plan in California to earn the highest possible quality-of-care rating—four stars—for eight consecutive years from the Office of the Patient Advocate. Kaiser Permanente has received countless other top accolades, including a perfect 5-out-of-5 rating from both the Centers for Medicare and Medicaid Services and the

NCQA Health Insurance Plan Ratings. Nationally they are widely considered the crème de la crème of healthcare excellence, alongside the Mayo Clinic.

Yet, when I was a young man growing up in Southern California in the 1960s and 1970s, Kaiser Permanente had a reputation as a bottom-of-the-barrel healthcare group when it came to quality care. The joke was "You go into Kaiser Permanente, but you don't come out!"

How was this enormous transformation accomplished? How did the worst become the best?

The answer can be summed up in one powerful word: purpose!

I have spoken for thousands of companies around the world, and virtually all of them talk about the importance of quality service and care for their customers, patients, and clients. But nowhere have I seen an organization more fanatical, focused, and consistent about delivering unexpected quality care than Kaiser Permanente. As Peter Drucker said so brilliantly, "Culture eats strategy for breakfast." At Kaiser Permanente, patient care is not a strategy; it is the driving force, the lifeblood, of every team member who works there. Quality patient care at Kaiser Permanente is the centerpiece for every decision. It is about the walk and not the talk. As a result, tremendous patient care has become the heartbeat of the organization, the DNA of the Kaiser Permanente culture.

It is this extraordinary focus on their purpose of delivering superb patient care that has made the difference. It has even enhanced their definition of patient. At Kaiser Permanente family members are viewed as patients every bit as much as those receiving care. Often the patients being treated are more concerned about the fears and worries of their loved ones than about themselves. When the patients see their family members being looked after warmly and attentively, it lifts their spirits and eases their tensions, so they are in a stronger state of mind and energy to deal with their own treatments.

When I worked extensively with the Kaiser Permanente West Los Angeles MCH (Mother-Child Healthcare) team, this devotion to extraordinary patient care led us to develop a simple but powerful way to personalize that focus so that every team member took full ownership of that purpose. We coined the term "the 4 W's," and it became the mechanism with which the team took their patient care results to the highest level.

The first W stands for *welcome*. Every interaction with patients and their families is seen as a WOO to create a welcoming energy. The MCH team became inspired to make sure that every patient and family member felt they had come to the right place. They created an environment that welcomed patients and their families in every way, focusing on every detail: physical layout, signage, and traffic flow throughout the medical center; smiling and helpful greetings wherever they went; proactive and conscientious communication delivered from staff, nurses, physicians, and midwives.

The welcome spirit went even further. Just as it was vital to provide welcoming energy to the patients and their families, it was also important for team members to extend a sense of welcome to one another. This changed the way the day shift and night shift interacted as they prepared to take over for each other. The result was no drop-off in the welcoming focus. Patients are very aware and sensitive to the way teammates engage one another. When they see real collaboration and appreciation among the staff, they feel even more confident that they will receive first-class care.

The second W stands for *warmth*. With a heightened focus on warmth, Kaiser Permanente MCH team members are constantly reminded that patients and their families are first and foremost human beings, not numbers, and that they are in the business of delivering care, not merely performing procedures. Fatigue, pain, worry, and emotion are the norm on the childbirth floor. Though the nurses and physicians have taken part in hundreds or even thousands of births, for patients and their loved ones it is new, unfamiliar, and often scary. It is the warmth of every single Kaiser Permanente MCH team member that eases that tension and uncertainty for patients. Warmth is perhaps most important when patients are the most emotional, worried, or unreasonable. Their focus on warmth means that team members are difficult to offend; they replace defensiveness with genuine compassion and kindness.

The third W is absolutely crucial to delivering truly exceptional care. It stands for *we*. As in every organization, there are many moving parts within the MCH function. When the day shift hands off patients to the night shift, it is extremely important that there is no drop-off in care, in particular in the first two W's. If 90 percent of a patient's experience is excellent but 10 percent is less than acceptable, odds are it is the unsatisfactory 10 percent that the patient will talk about and remember. *We* means that the team replaces ego with *we*-go, remembering that there can be no withholding information from others to try to look better than a teammate. Within MCH there are three main departments: delivery, postpartum, and the neonatal intensive care unit (NICU). As within many organizations, silos can develop among the various functional groups, separating and isolating them. When we shifted our focus to *we* at Kaiser Permanente West LA MCH, one fundamental question transformed silos into synergy. I asked all three functional groups, "Who is more important to patients?" Immediately the answer became obvious: *all* are equally important to the total patient experience. The delivery team brings the miracle of a new child to the world. The postpartum team teaches the new mother and family members how to care for their miracle. The NICU is there ready to jump into action if there are complications for either mother or baby.

By seeing themselves as *we*, the Kaiser Permanente MCH team looked at every patient as "our patient" and developed a deeper level of genuine appreciation for the talents, focus, and importance of every single team member. It generated a perspective that embraced collaboration and cohesion.

Finally, the fourth W stands for *wonderful*. This is the ultimate desired outcome, and it is the automatic result of successfully delivering the first three W's. The central vision for every MCH team member is to deliver such extraordinary care that patients describe their experience at Kaiser Permanente in one powerful word: *wonderful*. This is the shared purpose of every Kaiser Permanente MCH team member, the fuel for their inspiration.

The 4 W's created a simple and actionable focus to fulfill Kaiser Permanente team members' purpose of delivering sensational patient care. At every daily meeting the 4 W's were spotlighted, with special recognition given to team members who demonstrated excellence in delivering any of the W's. With this clear vision, the team consistently generated the highest patient care scores in their history. They came to work each day with a bit more bounce in their step and spark in their spirit. They had more fun, felt more appreciation for one another, and delivered truly inspired performance. They no longer viewed moments of adversity with frustration, but rather as WOOs to turn lemons into lemonade. That is the real magic of purpose for both individuals and teams, for when we are not inspired we are on the way to being expired. The choice is ours.

A WOO for You

When we hear, we forget; when we see, we remember; but when we *do*, we understand. I raised the questions below earlier in the chapter. I believe they will have tremendous value for you—but only if you truly think about and reflect on them. Spend some quiet time thinking about each question. When your answers become clear, you will accelerate your understanding of purpose in your life. By taking action in that direction, you will unleash your passion and energy.

1. What would you do if you knew you couldn't fail?

2. What makes you completely lose track of time and forget to eat, and causes all your aches, pains, and discomfort to magically disappear?

3. For what do you want to be remembered?

4. What did your eight-year-old self dream of?

5. What have been your greatest successes and biggest failures in your life?

6. What brings you the greatest joy and makes you feel the most alive?

7. What are you best at? What are your strengths?

8. What do you have an insatiable desire to learn more about?

9. What truly catches your attention and ignites your emotion?

10. In the past, what has captured your heart and brought tears of elation, inspiration, and passion to you?

Be Easy to Impress and Hard to Offend

In a world filled with so many WOOs, why do so many of us miss out on so much possibility and happiness? How can we rediscover the joy that bubbled out of us so easily when we were children? A WOO of the greatest magnitude and a can't-miss recipe for joy and connection is to become *easy to impress and hard to offend*. Those who are difficult to impress miss out on so much delight and wonder. And so much defensiveness, resentment, and missed WOOs result for those who are easily offended.

My grandmother Ruby was the best example I've ever known of a person who was always ready to be impressed and delighted. Her secret was that she looked for the light—and since what we focus on is what we create, she found wonder in everything. She was an extraordinary WOO-seizer.

A trip to the supermarket with Ruby was like a treasure hunt. When she found a beautiful ripe piece of fruit in the produce section she could hardly hold back her enthusiasm. She was so excited by the deals she would get with her coupons. And as we checked out, she always managed to find something to compliment about the other people in line, the clerk scanning her purchases, or the helper who bagged her groceries. She made their days brighter. She walked into the store with a grocery list but always emerged with friends and treasures. That's a person who is easy to impress.

When those around us sense that we are delighted and impressed by them, how does it make them feel? Instantly they feel valued and significant. And I've found that they in turn treat others with greater kindness, interest, and enthusiasm. When we choose to focus on the light, as Ruby did, we ignite an upward spiral of happiness and connection. We also become much harder to offend.

Golfing legend Jack Nicklaus is a great example of the long-term impact of being hard to offend. When Nicklaus first emerged on the golfing scene he immediately shook the status quo by beating the undisputed fan favorite, Arnold Palmer. This certainly didn't win him a lot of fans; in fact, he was reviled by many. Nicklaus was portrayed as the bad guy, an undeserving upstart who had no business challenging the beloved Palmer. Most of the venom spewed at Nicklaus had nothing to do with his talent, but rather attacked his appearance, personality, and style. It was unfair and mean-spirited.

But Nicklaus refused to be offended. He simply went about his game with great dignity, effort, and class. He gave credit to others and took responsibility for his own actions and performance no matter the outcome.

By being difficult to offend and by patiently holding to his principles, Nicklaus gradually saw the tide of public opinion turn, despite the fact that he and Palmer continued to be one of golf's greatest rivalries for more than a decade. Today he is revered even more for the quality of his character than for his unmatched accomplishments on the golf course. He has lived an extraordinary life in part because he refused to be offended.

Nicklaus has taught us a powerful lesson: no one can offend us without our permission. We always have a choice about our reaction and response. If we allow ourselves to be offended, we will live much of our lives on the defensive. As Mike and the Mechanics said so perfectly in their song "The Living Years," "We all talk a different language, talking in defense."

If I could undo anything in my life, it would be the moments when I allowed myself to be offended and struck back at others I love with defensiveness and anger. I believe that the love we fail to share is the only pain we live with. When we become easy to impress and hard to offend, we hold the secret to living more pain-free.

In business, being difficult to offend is a powerful secret to transforming negative customer feedback and criticism into WOOs to exceed expectations and generate loyalty.

My literary agent, Margret McBride, told me of an experience she had that demonstrated the impact of a business that has instilled the principle of being difficult to offend into the heart of their culture. On one of her many trips to New York City to meet with publishers, Margret decided to dine one evening at Eleven Madison Park, which was located near her hotel. She had been so consumed in meetings all day that she had not thought to make a reservation. So she simply walked over to the restaurant hoping there would be a table available. As she entered, it was clear that the place was extremely popular. In fact, it was packed. When she asked if there was any chance they could squeeze her in as a party of one, she expected to be told that there was no way.

But the response from the hostess surprised and delighted

her, and gave her an inkling that this was a very unusual place. The hostess said that though they were completely booked for the entire evening, she would create a small extra table just for Margret. In a matter of seconds she was escorted to a lovely little table they seemed to have pulled out of nowhere.

Her server greeted Margret as if she were a movie star, and described the various specials with such enthusiasm and delight she wanted to try every one. Her salad was exquisite and the wine superb. When her entrée arrived, however, though it was beautifully presented and obviously prepared with the finest ingredients, Margret found it too salty for her taste. She had been so famished, though, that she ate nearly half of it before deciding it just wasn't right for her. Here is where Margret became so amazed at the reaction of her server that she instantly became a raving fan of Eleven Madison Park.

When Margret explained that her entrée was too salty for her liking, the server didn't make an excuse, didn't defend the kitchen, didn't even merely apologize. Instead, he actually thanked Margret. He explained that without honest feedback, the restaurant could never be extraordinary. They viewed such feedback as WOOs to improve and better serve their customers. They were committed to pleasing every guest beyond their expectation. He helped her decide on another choice, which she absolutely loved. When Margret finished what had become a magnificent, memorable dining experience, her server surprised her once again. As he presented the check, he explained that at Eleven Madison Park they do not accept gratuities. Instead, all employees see themselves as owners committed to creating a dining environment that is second to none. They share that purpose and the success that comes from it. They are driven by what they can give rather than focusing on what they will get.

The next morning Margret couldn't wait to tell me all about her remarkable experience at Eleven Madison Park. Since then I'm certain she has told dozens of other friends and clients about it. It is little wonder that Eleven Madison Park has become one of the hottest restaurants in New York City. Because they have built a culture and spirit where criticism does not offend or ignite defensiveness, they have built a business that impresses beyond expectation.

A WOO for You

Imagine what would happen if as you headed into work today, you said to yourself: "Today I choose to be easy to impress and to look for and appreciate the best in others." And imagine if, as you head home, you repeated that same statement. What if you listened to your loved ones with rapt attention? What if you followed up with questions to show how curious you are about what they do and what they think? How would they feel if you noticed their light, and freed them to let it shine?

The next time you feel offended or attacked, ask yourself these questions: "What else could this mean? What don't I know about this situation?" The questions can open you to the possibility that something outside of you might be going on—information you don't yet have. Perhaps your being upset was simply a misunderstanding that could easily be cleared up if cooler heads prevail.

What do you think would happen if you calmly asked questions, instead of reacting to what you assume is going on?

7

The Power of
Asking Questions

In many of my talks I have attendees participate in an activity that I call a "blind date." After asking everyone to find a partner, I distribute blindfolds to each pair. The instructions are simple. For four minutes one of the partners in each pair is to be blindfolded. During those four minutes the other partner serves as their seeing-eye guide. They are free to move about wherever they choose. When the four minutes are up, they reverse roles wherever they are. After eight minutes they are to come back to the room where they started.

I next lay out three instructions for the guides during the four minutes they are leading their blindfolded partners:

1. They are to help their dates discover more of the world around them than they would see with their eyes open.

2. They are to make the experience for their blind dates fun, creative, outrageous, and enriching.

3. They are to take great care of their blind dates.

With those instructions, away they go. What happens next reveals a great deal about how we have been taught and conditioned to lead others, handle uncertainty, and build trust. It clearly, and often humorously, demonstrates how most of us have been programmed to focus on obstacles rather than WOOs. When the dust clears, the blind date exercise can open our eyes to the delight, adventure, and expansion of thinking that await us when we toss out that old teaching.

Within seconds after I send them off, the blindfolded partners discover something vital to know about themselves: do they or do they not trust the other person? The first time I experienced the blind date as a participant, I was certain that my perfectly nice partner was going to lead me to an open manhole or walk me into a wall. I did not trust. After having thousands of people participate in the blind date experience over the past twenty-five years, it has become clear that most people are like me. Filled with trepidation, they squeeze the blood out of their partner's arm as they inch ahead, certain they are about to bump into someone or something. Gradually, as they move through their four minutes, they let go of some of the fear. But most are very happy when their blindfolded time is up and they get to switch to the role of the guide.

When I thought about my blind date experience and my lack of trust, I realized that I was living my life precisely the same way. I was petrified of adventure and of the unknown. All I envisioned were obstacles, fears, and worries, rather than WOOs. The result was that I stayed frozen in my comfort zones even though deep down inside I knew they were actually imprisonment zones. My lack of trust kept me from looking for new relationships, from pursuing my dreams of writing, speaking, and growing as a person. By being blindfolded for the first time, I realized that I wanted to flip this conditioned lack of trust into openness and enthusiasm about new possibilities.

Participants experience another powerful aha moment when

I ask them about their experience of the world during the time they were blindfolded, as they began to trust more. They realized that as they let go of their fear of the obstacles and trusted their guides more, their other senses came alive. They noticed smells and sounds around them that had been completely blocked when all they felt was worry and doubt. Even their feet gave them new information, as they could sense different flooring as they moved to other rooms. They noticed subtle differences in temperature. Over the years, the more I observed the blind date activity, the more it became clear that when we are in a state of distrust, all we see are our fears about what could go wrong. The more we trust, the more we see, hear, smell, and feel.

Next we talk about what the participants learned from serving as guides. When they were thrust into leadership positions as the guides, they instantly felt a heightened sense of responsibility for their blindfolded partners. The real surprise comes when I ask them where they *focused* their responsibility. Almost without exception the guides directed their leadership and responsibility to the third instruction: to take great care of their blindfolded partners. Very few aim at helping them discover more of the world than they would have with their eyes open and to make the experience incredibly fun, creative, outrageous, and enriching.

By focusing solely on taking care of their blindfolded partners—on protecting them from harm—the guides lose sight of the other two instructions. They move much more slowly, avoid any risks, and simply try to get their dates through the four minutes without incident. They tell their dates exactly where they are and describe everything that's coming their way.

As we review the experience together it becomes apparent

that by concentrating only on taking care of their dates, the guides don't give their dates all the gifts inherent in the other two instructions—discovery, fun, creativity, and enrichment. But when you think about it, isn't this is the way most of us have been taught to live life? Though we think we are protecting others and taking care of them, we're actually keeping them from discovery, fun, creativity, and enrichment. We are taught to move through life looking out for what could go wrong instead of what could go right. As Abraham Lincoln put it, "The worst things we can do for a person are the things he could and should do for himself."

For those few guides who focus their responsibility on discovery and enrichment, the blindfolded partner's experience is completely different. These guides demonstrate what happens when we focus on looking for the WOOs. I can spot these pairs right away, because they tend to laugh more and have a faster pace as the guide seeks to totally engage their blindfolded partner. These are the pairs for whom I must really watch the time, because if I don't tell them when their four minutes are up, they will just keep going. Perhaps the biggest difference between these guides and the others is that they *ask* more than *tell*.

It took me perhaps fifty times of leading the blind date activity in my events before I realized that very few of the guides asked questions of their blindfolded partners. They were too busy describing what was happening. The only question I heard occasionally was "What do you think this is?" when they had their blindfolded partner touch an object. Then, during one blind date, I heard a guide ask, "What color is this?" At first I laughed at the question, but then I realized how brilliant this guide was. By asking such an unexpected question, she had caused her date to really think, intuit, and explore.

What happens when we ask more than tell? What impact does it have on those around us?

It's exciting to recognize that through questions, we help others discover new possibilities and to think creatively. We help them feel significant and important. By asking what they think, we teach them that their insights, ideas, and observations have real value. Ironically, through the power of questions we take far better care of them than when we are simply trying to protect them, because we prepare them to think for themselves and look for the WOOs.

Exciting possibilities come to light when we ask new and better questions—not only of others but ourselves. One simple question in particular helps us discover the WOO in situations that formerly created great angst. It's a surefire way to transform fear into freedom, and failure into faith. This simple question completely flipped my own trepidation into genuine enjoyment of a strategy that has had a tremendous positive impact on my career.

When my first book, *Beyond Success*, based on John Wooden's leadership principles, was published, I decided that appearing on talk radio shows would be a great way to promote the book. But when I first began appearing on the radio shows I was nervous and uneasy. I kept worrying about what could go wrong. What if the interviewer embarrassed me, or was sarcastic and negative about leadership and personal growth books? What if I froze up or became stumped by a question? But I remembered to ask myself a simple question: "What's great about this?" In an instant, I realized that by enthusiastically participating on these shows, I would be able to reach thousands of people with ideas that can help them live happy, fulfilling lives. What's more, I could speak to them in their cars and homes all over the country from the comfort of my home office, without having to leave my family. Suddenly I felt excited and grateful rather than anxious, and my performance improved dramatically.

That simple change in focus led me to ask myself another empowering question: "How can I do these interviews and have fun?" This question sparked a truly empowering new thought. Though I couldn't control the interviewer, I *could* control my own energy and enthusiasm. Before each interview I slapped a big grin on my face and took a few rich, full breaths. I bought a set of headphones, and instead of sitting motionless at my desk during the interview, I got up on my feet and walked around my office with energy. I created momentum instead of hesitation. Best of all, I began to thoroughly enjoy the interviews and see them as exciting WOOs.

Don't we all have important tasks and responsibilities so difficult or distasteful to us that we continually worry about them or put them off, even though we know how critical they are? In the face of them we tighten up with feelings of frustration ("I can't do this"), ineptitude ("I'm terrible at this"), or indignation ("Why do I have to do this?"). What would happen if the next time we encountered these obstacles, we saw them as *opportunities* to apply the transformative principle "If it's not working, try something different"? What if we asked ourselves new, empowering questions like "What's great about this?" or "How can I do this differently and have fun in the process?"

Asking these new questions will remind us to focus on the WOO, rather than settle because we're focusing on limitations. When we change our questions, we shoot up the 10-point energy scale and turn trepidation into acceleration. Why? Because fresh questions help us focus on purpose.

·   ·   ·

One of the most important areas in which we can apply the principle "If it's not working, try something different" is in the ratio of praise to criticism we communicate in our relationships both personally and professionally. Seizing this WOO can be remarkably healing, nurturing, and connecting.

When my oldest daughter, Kelsey, was ten years old, I fell into the bad habit of being excessively critical of her and chiding her about every little thing. One day I became so short with her when I was helping her with homework that she burst into tears.

My heart sank as I saw how much my criticism had crushed her. It jolted me back to my senses. Hugging her, I apologized from the bottom of my heart: "Kelsey, I am *so* sorry. You are so smart and you work so hard! I couldn't be more proud of you."

As her tears dried, she crawled into my lap and her sweet smile returned. I made up my mind to offer more praise than criticism—I was determined to lift her up, not tear her down. In the future, I would catch her doing things *right*!

So what is the optimal ratio of praise to criticism? Research conducted by Emily Heaphy, now at Boston University's Questrom School of Business, and Marcial Losada, now a consultant and formerly of the Center for Advanced Research in Ann Arbor, Michigan, concluded that in the business arena, high-performing teams (measured according to financial results, customer satisfaction ratings, and 360-degree employee feedback) averaged between five and six statements of praise for every one statement of criticism. Low-performing teams averaged three criticisms to a single statement of praise. This research was remarkably similar to John Gottman's study of married couples' likelihood of getting divorced or remaining married, where the single biggest determining factor proved to be the ratio of positive to negative comments the partners make *to* one another. In Gottman's research the optimal ratio was almost identical: five statements of praise for every one criticism.

During my years as vice president of performance planning for an international transportation company, our San Francisco office had been ravaged by conflict between operations and sales. Turnover was horrific and morale nearly nonexistent. When we promoted our Hawaii assistant operations manager to the position of operations head in San Francisco, I'll never forget what she told me in her interview: "Brian, my goal is simple. I want everyone on the San Francisco team, whether in operations or sales, to know that I am completely loyal to them. Once they know that's true, I am certain we will come together as a team and make great progress."

Claire had inherited a night operations manager with a reputation for being extremely difficult to work with: gruff, antagonistic, and quick to blame others. But Claire refused to listen to the past. When we suggested to her that perhaps it would be best to replace him, she replied, "Give me a chance to work with him. He is so talented and experienced, I know that when he feels supported he will respond."

Claire made a conscious effort to look beyond the manager's past reputation, and instead praised him for his operational knowledge and expertise. She asked for his input and suggestions about major proposals and made sure to give him credit when she relayed these ideas to the San Francisco sales manager. Within twelve months after Claire came to San Francisco, the station had nearly doubled their previous revenue and had become solidly profitable, and the night ops manager we had been sure needed to be let go had been chosen by the combined operations and sales managers from our entire system as the outstanding operations employee of the quarter.

When you establish fierce loyalty to each member of your team through a positive ratio of praise to criticism, you instill a culture of mutual support, respect, and commitment to extraordinary service and performance. You become a catalyst of construction rather than destruction. You build loyalty by *being* loyal! When you change the way you look at people, the people you look at change, too!

Start today to change the ratio of praise to criticism in your work and home. Look for the positive qualities, efforts, and actions of others, and express appreciation and admiration. Catch others doing things right. Try something different. The instant you do, you will have opened a new WOO.

A WOO for You

Have you ever heard from an old friend or colleague out of the blue who wanted to tell you how much you meant to them? How did this unexpected connection make you feel?

How would you like to try something different today and proactively give someone else the same gift of praise by emailing, texting, sending a handwritten card, instant messaging on Facebook, or calling someone whom you haven't thanked for their impact on your life?

This simple action may become one of the most fulfilling WOOs you've ever seized.

BUILD PEOPLE, BUILD TEAMS, BUILD RELATIONSHIPS

8

The Positive Pygmalion

Have you ever thought about the impact our thoughts, beliefs, and expectations have on others? Through a phenomenon known as the Pygmalion effect, we are able to move, nudge, or pull those around us in another direction almost invisibly by how we think about them, what we expect from them, and what we believe they are capable of. The term was derived from the story from Greek mythology about a sculptor from the island of Cyprus named Pygmalion who poured so much of his passion into a statue of a woman he carved from stone that he fell deeply in love with it. The goddess of love, Aphrodite, was so struck by Pygmalion's love for his creation that she descended to earth and fired a magical arrow into the heart of the sculpture, instantly transforming the stone into a living, breathing woman named Galatea. Together she and Pygmalion lived happily ever after.

Every great teacher, coach, and leader has mastered the Pygmalion effect, the principle that our thoughts, beliefs, and expectations can change others almost magnetically. Whether conscious or unconscious, these great leaders are able to convey belief in others at key moments that can flip the switch of possibility for them and shoot their lives off in entirely new trajectories.

When I was a freshman in high school my guidance counselor, Mr. Anderson, called me into his office one morning. Looking unusually serious, he said, "Brian, a student like you only comes along about once every ten or fifteen years."

Now, the truth was, when he said it there was a really good chance he meant it more in a bad way than in a good way. While I was doing pretty well in my coursework, all I really cared about was goofing around, hoping that everyone would think I was funny and cool. I was that kid you remember from high school who couldn't wait to interrupt class with a joke or some smart-alecky remark. Deep down inside, I was just scared. I desperately wanted everyone to like me.

Somehow Mr. Anderson saw through all that. And the next words he said changed my life. "There's something special in you, Brian. Stop wasting it! Every day is a gift. But only if you open it. You haven't opened one. Stop messing around and being afraid to try your best. Put your heart into your life. Stand up tall and be the student, leader, and person I know you can be."

Even more important than Mr. Anderson's words that day was the way he said them. He wasn't interested in appealing to my intellect; he was committed to reaching into my heart. The impact was like Aphrodite's arrow.

Looking back now, I'm certain that had he not said those words to me that morning so long ago, I never would have worked hard enough to have been accepted into Stanford University. Had I not gone to Stanford, I never would have discovered my passion for coaching, which led me eventually to my search for balance, which ultimately brought me to my wife and daughters and a wonderful life.

Mr. Anderson believed in me more than I believed in myself, and when he had the chance to express his expectations, he seized that WOO. That's what *positive* Pygmalions do!

It was in my years as a swimming coach that I had the unforgettable experience of working with an athlete who took the lesson that Mr. Anderson had taught me to a whole new level: only when we see the *best* in others do we have the chance to inspire it. Positive Pygmalions look for strengths and WOOs; negative Pygmalions see only weaknesses and obstacles.

Throughout his swimming career, Ron was the kind of young man who caused coaches to shake their heads in disappointment and throw their hands up in frustration. Blessed with a great personality and considerable natural ability but seemingly little grit or determination, he skated by, never digging deep to bring out his true potential. His attendance at practice was as unpredictable as the weather. Just when you'd begin to think he had turned the corner in his commitment, he would disappear for days at a time, negating any progress he'd made in conditioning and focus. Though he had enough talent to do well even with his halfhearted effort, he simply didn't seem to care that much.

Ron joined my team when he and the rest of his former club merged with ours to create a real swimming powerhouse. I had seen him at meets over the years and knew of both his talent and his reputation for lackluster training habits. What I didn't know when he walked onto the pool deck that September afternoon was that buried beneath Ron's happy-go-lucky exterior beat the heart of a champion. There was a spirit of passion and energy within him just aching to come out. He was just frightened and hiding from his potential, like so many of us do.

What if he gave his best and it wasn't good enough? What if he committed himself and failed? It was so much easier to amble along on talent alone, protected by the invisible comfort zone called "unrealized potential."

Ron's past coaches had tried to needle him into caring, calling him a loafer and a waste of talent—a strategy that clearly did not work over the long term. Occasionally he would respond with an "I'll show you!" effort, but quickly he would slide back even further into his blasé attitude.

I have never believed in sarcasm as a motivator because the energy it evokes comes from embarrassment, fear, or revenge. These emotions can generate short-term results but not long-term inspiration. From the moment Ron joined our team, I focused on his potential and praised him for every effort that moved him a little closer to it. I wanted to be a positive influence for Ron, and so I left his past behavior in the past, understanding fully that what we focus on is what we create. I knew how important it is to see what's possible in people, even when they don't see it themselves.

After his first week with the team, Ron came to me after practice one afternoon and said, "Coach, I'm having fun here. I've never felt like someone believed in me as much as you do."

I responded, "Ron, you've been a joy to have here this week. You've got everything it takes to be the California Interscholastic Federation champion if you decide it's something you truly want. The greatest fun in life is to put your heart and soul on the line one hundred percent and to discover what's really inside of you. I do believe in you, and I'm really excited that you've joined our team."

He smiled and turned just a tad red. But I could see the positive impact of the faith I had expressed in him far overpowered any embarrassment he felt at receiving such compliments.

After that talk, Ron became a dream to train. In all my years of coaching, never had I worked with an athlete who tried harder and had more fun doing it. Ron made the decision to go for it; he attacked his senior year of swimming, placing his full faith in me and in himself. On the rare occasions when he didn't have his A-game, he never let his positive spirit dissipate. As a result, he had few subpar days and bounced back from any disappointment almost immediately. More than any swimmer with whom I'd ever had the pleasure to work, Ron looked inside himself to determine his success, rather than evaluating his ability according to what everyone else thought, or on the basis of one poor performance. Even on days when he didn't turn in his fastest practice times, he was able to feel good about his effort. With this fresh spirit Ron improved dramatically.

By the time the high school season began, Ron was performing workout sets and drills I had never seen accomplished before. And he obviously enjoyed every minute of it. He came to practice each day with a smile on his face and a twinkle in his eye that seemed to say, *Come on, Coach, let's see what we can do today.* Where years of the negative Pygmalion staples of sarcasm and ridicule had left him uninspired and uncommitted, he responded to praise and positive energy with boundless enthusiasm.

His attitude and effort had quite an effect on the entire team. For the first time in his life, Ron knew what it felt like to be admired. He became our team leader by his extraordinary example. His enthusiasm was infectious, and all of the kids seemed to have more energy and worked harder while complaining less. Practices had never been so much fun.

It was hard to believe how swiftly the year flew by when we arrived at East Los Angeles City College for the California Interscholastic Federation High School Championship prelims. Ron was to swim three events—the 200-yard individual medley (50 yards of each of the four competitive strokes), the 100-yard backstroke, and a leg on his school's medley relay. With all my heart, I wanted this transformed young man to experience a moment of great triumph at the high school championships. He deserved no less.

The prelims were the qualifiers for the finals that would occur three days later. Because of his fine performances during the dual meet season, Ron was seeded in the top three in both of his individual events, though there was no clear favorite. The top swimmers were closely bunched, within a few tenths of a second of one another.

In the sport of swimming, top athletes train extremely hard. These determined kids rise each morning around four-thirty and hit the water by five for a two-hour workout before school. Then, after a full day in classes, they come back for an evening workout, another grueling two-hour test of stamina. On top of their endless hours in the pool, they lift weights four days a week. As a result, during the season, they are dead-tired. The entire training strategy points at one shining light at the end of an exhausting tunnel—the taper and peak period. This is the three weeks or so before the big meet when they stop morning practices and gradually reduce the intensity of their afternoon workouts. With the added rest, their muscles and spirits begin to rejuvenate, and they prepare psychologically and physically for their best performances. It is a very exciting time for a swimmer. With a couple of days to go before the target competition, the kids begin to feel so much energy they could pop.

The last big step is to "shave down." The night before the big meet, the kids shave the hair from their arms, legs, back, and stomach—some even shave their heads, though most opt for a cap or a short haircut. When they hit the water after shaving they feel incredible—it's as if they are suddenly lighter than air. It's an amazing sensation and a huge boost mentally and emotionally.

For the preliminaries, Ron and I decided that he would not shave down. Though it was slightly risky, we felt confident he would easily qualify in the top eight anyway, and then would have an extra edge when he shaved for the finals.

The day of the prelims finally arrived and we were psyched. Ron's goal for the 200-yard individual medley was 1:57.9, and I secretly hoped that he might go as fast as 1:55.9 in the finals if everything went perfectly. He had never broken 2:02 before, but we both were visualizing the best. In his preliminary heat he started off the race looking strong, but his timing seemed a bit off when he reached the breaststroke leg. The effort was there, but he tired as the race progressed and really struggled the last 25 yards. His time was 1:59.9, and though it was a personal best, I could see his disappointment when he came over to me to talk about the race. Indeed, I was worried, because he had really looked tired in the last half of the event, and the finals were only a few days away. He had worked so hard, and our hopes were so high. What if we had overestimated his ability? What if his goals were out of reach? As he looked to me for answers, I could sense a tinge of doubt creeping into his mind.

I did my very best to instill more confidence in him than I actually felt at that moment. I smiled at him and said with great conviction, "No worries. You're still three days away. When the finals come on Thursday, you're going to be awesome." Thank goodness he didn't know I was trying to solidify my own faith as much as his. True to the spirit he had shown all year long, he bounced right back as he listened to my pep talk, nodding at me with the twinkle back in those laughing eyes of his. He felt even better when we found out he had qualified first in the individual medley and second in the backstroke. But when we left the prelims that evening, I couldn't help but wonder if he was going to fall far short of his goals. He deserved his moment, and I prayed he would find something magical inside him by Thursday.

That week at our short practices, Ron was right back to his cheerful, upbeat self. We both knew Thursday would be his one big shot at his dreams. If he approached the goals we had set for him, he might catch the eye of a college recruiter or two, with an outside chance of a scholarship. He would be a hero at his school, single-handedly responsible for his school earning an unprecedented top-five finish in overall team points.

Wednesday afternoon, after a very light practice with a few sprints tossed in to rev the kids' engines, I asked Ron to come into my office for a talk. He had been in my thoughts incessantly and I wanted him to know how honored I felt to be his coach. I thanked him for all he had meant to me and told him that every day that season I looked forward to practice with extra enthusiasm knowing he was going to be there ready to meet every challenge with pure joy. As much as I had wanted to be a positive influence for him, he had been even more of one for me. I told him that no matter what he did the next day, to me he was already a champion in the truest sense.

"When you step up on those starting blocks tomorrow, remember how completely I believe in you. You deserve an amazing day and you are going to fly." I gave him a big bear hug and joked with him about remembering to put a blade in the razor when he shaved down that night. The last thing I said to him was, "Sleep well tonight. You can rest easy knowing that you could not have prepared any better. You're ready." As I watched Ron walk out to his car, I looked to God for help in making my prediction after his prelim swims clairvoyant rather than unrealistically optimistic.

The energy was electric at the East L.A. City College pool the next day. At that time southern California was the hotbed of swimming in the United States, and the CIF Championship was the premier high school swimming event in the world. School spirit was running rampant as cheers erupted from every corner of the aquatic center. Only the fastest eight swimmers in each event had survived the preliminaries to make it to these finals, and each and every competitor was primed to put it all on the line.

Because I was Ron's club team coach and not his high school coach, I was not allowed on the pool deck for this championship meet. Knowing of this restriction, we had carefully gone over his warm-up plan in advance. I positioned myself at the most visible spot in the bleachers, where Ron and all of my other swimmers could easily spot me. If it's possible to transmit energy and faith through space, from my perch up in the stands I sent my kids all I had as I watched them loosen up. Ron's first race, the 200-yard individual medley, would be one of the earliest events. His performance would quickly tell me if this would be a day of triumph or one of disappointment. I just hoped Ron wasn't as nervous as I was.

As he walked over to sit behind the starting blocks with the other seven competitors, Ron looked out at the end of the pool, deep in concentration. He was visualizing his race, just as he'd done a hundred times before. Each finalist stepped forward when introduced by the announcer and was greeted with a wild explosion of cheers. When Ron heard his name, he stepped up on the block and acknowledged the crowd with a wave, and then, spotting me, gave a quick nod as if to say, *I'm ready, Coach. I got this.* I smiled back and gave him a thumbs-up.

All cheering and last minute conversation came to an abrupt stop as the starter blew his whistle, the signal for total silence except for his instructions to the swimmers.

"Judges and timers ready . . . swimmers take your marks . . ." *Boom!* The gun went off, and eight peak-performance athletes exploded from the blocks, their legs driving like pistons as they stretched for the water. Ron had a terrific start, and after 25 yards he was already in the lead.

The first half of the race, consisting of the butterfly and backstroke legs, was his strongest, so I expected Ron to open up about a body length's lead. But when he hit the halfway mark I was stunned. He was flying. He was over two seconds ahead of the pace we had hoped for and had moved at least three full body lengths ahead of the second-place swimmer. But could he keep it up?

I held my breath as he made the turn into the breaststroke leg. This was where he had faltered on Monday, when his timing had fallen off and fatigue had crept into his arms and legs. But today he looked fantastic! He was on top of the water, driving forward with terrific thrust from his whip kick. I had never seen him swim with such power in the breaststroke before. My heart nearly pounded out of my chest as I watched this tremendous young man find the brilliance that had always been hidden inside of him. *Fifty yards of freestyle left to go,* I shouted in my mind. *Please let him finish strong.*

He turned for home, every muscle in his powerful body blasting toward the finish. With ten yards left, he put his head down and accelerated into the wall without breathing. His closest competitor was more than half a pool length behind him.

As soon as he hit the finish he whirled around to look up at the giant scoreboard clock that instantly flashed up his time: 1:53.86! He had both shattered the CIF record and exceeded our wildest dreams by more than two seconds. In the process, he had qualified for the most prestigious swimming meet in the United States, the Senior National Championships. We had never even considered that possibility.

As soon as he saw his time, he turned and looked for me in the stands. When our eyes connected he leaped out of the water to his waist and pumped his right arm toward the heavens in absolute joy and triumph. His huge smile was the greatest gift a coach could ever receive. The entire stadium was applauding wildly for him, and he flew out of the pool, forgetting all about my pre-race instructions to go straight into the warm-down pool and loosen up for his backstroke event. Instead, he rushed up the stairs, pumping his fists and howling in utter delight until he reached me. He wrapped his arms around me and lifted me right off the ground in a giant hug of pure exultation. The next second, his parents joined our unrestrained celebration. Goosebumps, tears, and gratitude flowed nonstop. A phenomenal young man had transformed his life and received the moment he truly deserved.

Ron went on to win the 100-yard backstroke as well, once again eclipsing the CIF record and demolishing his personal best time by more than two and a half seconds. To top it all off, he lifted his team on his powerful shoulders and carried them to a third-place finish in the team standings, by far the highest place they had ever achieved. Ron was named outstanding swimmer of the meet and received a full-scholarship offer from the University of Utah.

Ron's story of triumph and transformation that season mean more to me now than ever, for on the night he was inducted as the first swimmer ever into his high school's athletic hall of fame, Ron passed away from a sudden and massive heart attack. He was forty-seven years old.

The lessons he taught me about the power of the positive Pygmalion burn brighter than ever in my heart. Ron helped me see that whenever we give our most dedicated and determined efforts, our focus and actions will lead to extraordinary results, just as he experienced. Like Ron, we may not find instant gratification. Indeed, we may even wonder, as time goes on, if a lifetime of planting will ever result in a richly deserved harvest. But remember, faith has no time limit. The rewards for living as a positive Pygmalion for ourselves and others and focusing on possibility rather than limit cannot be denied. In simply making these important decisions and taking action we have already succeeded. The instant we know we are the best, it is ours. We experience joy that cannot be taken away. Through our choices, we discover the healing, freeing peace of mind that is faith in action.

A WOO for You

Who are the Rons in *your* life?

What would happen if you allowed Ron's story to inspire you to start today on the path to becoming a truly positive Pygmalion by flipping past patterns and consistently communicating what you *want*, rather than what you don't want?

When guiding others you might describe the desired outcome rather than telling them what *not* to do.

Instead of saying, "Don't forget," you could say, "Remember."

Rather than telling your children, "Don't leave your room so messy," you could encourage them by saying, "I love it when you leave your room looking nice."

In a short time you'll replace the don'ts in your life with dos, the "you can't" with "you can."

I believe you can break through the old conditioning you learned growing up and become the truly positive Pygmalion who elevates everyone around you. And as much as you are a Pygmalion to others, you are just as much a Pygmalion to yourself.

What would happen if you began to use the same new communication in your self-talk?

Why not build the unstoppable belief within yourself that you have choices in your life?

How would it feel to approach challenges, tasks, and change with a joyful "want to, like to, love to, choose to" attitude rather than the feeling that you "have to"?

How much difference would it make to put yourself at the cause, instead of the effect, and view each and every day as a gift and a WOO?

9

Take the High Road— The View Is So Much Better

What is the most destructive word in the language of teams and families? Whether it's with our family, our business, our friends, or within ourselves, that most destructive word is *blame*. Why is blame so harmful, and why does it serve no practical purpose? When you take a look at blame in the context of time, blame is always about the past. So whenever we stay in blame we're living in the past, a place where we have no chance to change.

And yet, just as we have never been taught to look for the WOO, most of us have been programmed to blame others. When you think of our political environment, for example, the proliferation of negative campaigning has turned election season into one big blame party. And isn't our legal system primarily based upon apportioning blame? Astonishingly, more than 90 percent of the world's lawsuits are filed in the United States, and every one of them is seeking to fix blame on someone else. We blame our parents for our insecurities, our children for not listening to us, conservatives for having no social conscience

and catering only to big business, and liberals for overregula-
tion and catering primarily to the poor. We blame the president for pretty much everything, and for whatever is left over
we blame Congress. On the highways we blame all those other
crazy drivers. But does blame bring us any lasting satisfaction
or happiness? Of course not! And its real damage is that blame
blocks us from seeing WOOs.

Isn't it time to move beyond all this negative conditioning and rise up to become blame-busters? Blame-busters ac-
knowledge that mistakes are made—even when we've made
them. But we refuse to stay locked in the past. We recognize
that often it is our missteps that guide us to a better path. The
WOOs, on the other hand, exist in the present. It is *right now.*
So if we are to seize them, we must move beyond the past. And
we'll be glad we did—the view is so much better from the high
road.

In 2014, one of the big stories in sports was that LeBron
James, the greatest basketball player in the world at the time,
was returning home to play for the Cleveland Cavaliers. As
huge as this story was to basketball fans, it was an even more
important story of forgiveness and blame busting.

When James had made the decision to leave Cleveland four
years earlier to play for the Miami Heat, he was reviled by
Cavalier fans, and absolutely lambasted by the team's owner,
Dan Gilbert. In a public letter published in the Cleveland
newspaper at the time, Gilbert attacked James's character and
integrity. He called LeBron cowardly, narcissistic, and a hor-
rible role model for young people.

But when LeBron realized that his heart was back home
in Ohio, he opened the door to Gilbert through the power of
forgiveness and said, "Who am I to hold a grudge?" He owned
up to his mistakes about the overblown way he originally an-

nounced his decision to join the Heat, accepting responsibility for the past but focusing on the WOO in front of him. Gilbert also fully accepted responsibility for his childish, bitter, and inappropriate remarks. Both admitted that if they had the chance to do it over, they would have acted differently. By being blame-busters, James and Gilbert ignited new and exciting possibilities. They stood together as LeBron announced he was coming home, determined to give long-suffering Cleveland a championship. In his first year back, despite several injuries to key teammates, LeBron led the Cavaliers to the NBA Finals and brought fresh new hope to Cleveland. One year later that hope was made manifest as LeBron and his teammates brought Cleveland its first professional sports title in fifty-two years.

Think of the enormous positive impact we have on our teammates when, as blame-busters, we accept the responsibility to change and improve *ourselves* when things are not going well. When we keep to the high road we become examples that inspire better performances and build commitment. The legendary Alabama football coach Paul "Bear" Bryant explained the impact of blame busting in his down-home style when he said, "I'm just a country plow-hand, but I've learned to get a team beating with one heart: If anything goes great, *they* did it. If anything goes semi-good, *we* did it. If anything goes real bad, *I* did it." When we live by Bryant's sage advice, we'll inspire loyalty rather than backstabbing, and teamwork instead of selfishness.

What feelings and emotions are generated within others—whether teammates, family, friends, or customers—when we sincerely and unselfishly accept responsibility for errors and decisions that meant we didn't achieve desired results? Instantly others rally around us. Past problems and mistakes have now been accounted for, and they are free to let go of the past and move forward to tackle the present and future. Our teammates respect our courage, honesty, and willingness to express human fallibility. As we demonstrate genuine humility, we motivate others to seek win-win solutions rather than to waste valuable energy seeking a target for their frustration and fear. The moment we say, "I am responsible. I didn't do a good enough job," or "I made a poor decision," or "I did not come through for you," the uncertainty that fuels the upset is over. Then, when we honestly express our commitment to improve our performance, others are ready to renew their support and optimism.

But what about blaming ourselves? When we accept responsibility for our actions that have not produced the results we sought, it's equally important not to blame ourselves either, for blame is just as destructive within us as it is focused outside. What would happen if we simply accepted the reality that new and different actions are necessary? Suddenly we can see that although our efforts and motives may have been well-intended, change is required to create success. We can move forward and stop beating ourselves up. When our new actions create better results, we can give credit and praise to others without hesitation. Responsibility is something we take, especially during the tough times; credit is something we give whenever we see the WOO.

Years ago I had the opportunity to teach a two-and-a-half-day seminar for a special group of young people in Fort Worth, Texas. The kids selected for the seminar were high school seniors who had failed to pass a basic competency examination required for graduation in the state of Texas. In fact, these kids had failed the test four times. The maximum number of opportunities students were given to pass the test was five. They were down to their last chance. The exam was scheduled about three weeks after our weekend seminar for the kids.

The program I designed for these young people was aimed at helping them break through negative conditioning, fear, and destructive habits that kept them in the viselike grip of failure. Through games, experiential activities, and stories, my goal was to replace doubt with confidence, indifference with determination. I had taught the course in each of the previous two years with exciting results, so I expected the best. The seminar is vibrant, fun, and activating. Rather than lecturing to the kids, I involve them in experiences that are surprising, thought-provoking, and inspiring.

But as I began to work with this particular group, I could see I was in for a major challenge. It was immediately apparent to me that these kids were bright enough to pass the test. They were creative, quick-thinking, and energetic—as long as they weren't in the classroom. As soon as they were asked to be attentive and to learn, however, they shut down. At first I thought they just didn't care. But then I began to see they were simply afraid. Subconsciously they had resigned themselves to failure. The easy way out was to give up without even trying. They could then slough the whole thing off with a convenient rationalization: "I could have passed the test if I wanted to. It just wasn't any big deal."

The more I tried to involve the kids and build enthusiasm, the more they pushed back—not by being aggressive, but rather by mentally checking out. Not once in hundreds of seminars had I encountered a group so disconnected and unmotivated. The physical participation, fun, and heart in the program had always won over even the most skeptical teams. But these kids were yawning, falling asleep, and paying zero attention.

As I struggled through the first day, I began to get frustrated with the kids, despite my best intentions. I felt the negative energy of blame beginning to take hold of my spirit. Luckily, just as my frustration was starting to escalate into anger, I arrived at the section in the seminar that focused on blame busting. I remembered that the meaning of my communication is the response I generate. Since I wasn't generating the response I wanted, I decided to take a risk.

When we finished a game that is designed to point out the futility of blame, I stepped forward and got right in the kids' faces. They had sleepwalked through the game with their typical indifference. Up until this point I had met every yawn with patience and kindness. But now I stared icily into their eyes and said in a stern, almost menacing voice, "You know, I came two thousand miles, spending four days away from my wife and children, to be here with you. And you're not getting a thing from it."

As I scolded the kids I watched their reaction closely. It was exactly what I had hoped for. A couple of them nudged one another with a hint of a smile, as if to say, *We're getting to him. He's losing it.* They *wanted* me to give up on them and leave them alone. Then they would have an airtight excuse to give up on themselves. They could just mess around for the rest of the time and pin the worthlessness of the seminar on the teacher who lost his cool.

Encouraged by their response, I became even more intense. I said, "It would be so easy for me right now to say, 'What's *wrong* with you?'" Once again I could sense the growing feeling among the kids that I had indeed lost it and would soon be out of their hair.

But what I said next shocked them: "It would be so easy for me to blame you for not caring about anything important. *But if I did that, I'd be dead wrong!*"

Several of the kids did double-takes and looked at me as if to ask, *Huh? What did he say?*

Impassioned, I went on, "There are ideas, principles, and possibilities in this class that can do more than help you pass that test in three weeks so you can walk across the stage on graduation day. There is value here that can change your life! But you're not getting it because I haven't been a good enough teacher to help you see. If I blamed you, I'd be dead wrong. If you're not finding the value that's right here today, I can't blame you, I've got to change *me*!"

For the first time in our more than six hours together, every eye in the room was glued to me. They weren't used to having someone take responsibility for their attitudes and indifference. They were used to being blamed. Suddenly they were confused, but interested and attentive.

I next told them a story about one of my dearest friends who broke free from addiction to cocaine through the unconditional love and support of an intervention team. It is an intense, emotional story I rarely tell in my seminars. I had not planned to share the story with the kids, but at that moment my intuition told me it was the right thing to do. As I told the story you could have heard a pin drop in the room. Every one of those kids was right with me, hanging on every word. I saw several of them choke up with emotion. I realized that here was a story with which they could identify. They had seen more drugs, violence, and fear in their seventeen or eighteen years than most people see in a lifetime. When I finished telling the story, something happened I will never forget. One by one those kids stood up and gave me a standing ovation.

Ten minutes earlier I'd been on the verge of losing them. Had I chosen blame, I surely would have, for when we focus on blame we block out all WOOs. Later, each of the students broke a one-inch-thick wooden board karate style as a personal metaphor for breaking through. On the front of the board they wrote about a fear, habit, or obstacle they were determined to move beyond in their lives. On the other side of the board they described the feelings, accomplishments, and positive changes they would create for themselves and those they loved when they successfully broke through. The support and energy in the room during board breaking flew right off the charts!

About two months later I received a letter from one of the kids, Tanesha, telling me that she and almost all of the others had passed the test. She wrote, "When we were taking the test we brought along our broken boards. Now we are ready to graduate in May. Even the ones that didn't pass made improvement. We are very thankful to you for encouraging us to think positive and to believe in ourselves. Without you pushing us on, I don't think we would have made it. Thank you."

In business, leaders who embrace responsibility and refuse to blame circumstances or team members strengthen the resilience, creativity, and energy to challenge and disrupt the status quo.

Shortly after I came aboard the executive team at Lynden Air Freight we faced an enormous challenge. For many years we had been the key air freight forwarder between the lower forty-eight U.S. states and Alaska. But seemingly overnight that market had dried up to a trickle because oil production in Alaska had suddenly stopped as a result of a major decrease in the price of oil.

With sales and profitability down and our future in doubt, blame, defensiveness, and finger pointing threatened to infect our organization. Our parent company made it clear we needed to turn things around and fast. We were quickly approaching panic mode.

When the president of our company suddenly called us together for an emergency meeting, we all expected him to deliver tough news about layoffs and salary cuts. But in one powerful statement he shifted our focus from constriction to expansion, from crisis to opportunity. He took us all by surprise when he stood up and said, "This is a great day! Though I understand the fear and paralysis that I sense throughout the company and from everyone in this room, this is the perfect opportunity for us to redefine who we are and break away from the status quo. We can seize this opportunity to do things we never dreamed of before. Who do we really want to be?"

Instantly he shifted the mood in the room from fear to freedom, from failure to faith. He activated our resilience and energy. With the weight of blame lifted from our shoulders, ideas flew fast and furious during the rest of that meeting, and we emerged excited about our possibilities.

Within a year we had established ourselves as a major player in the Hawaiian market, nearly doubled our domestic business, and become one of the leading shippers of fine art. Within two years we had risen to the top of our industry for service excellence, added hundreds of jobs, and established consistent bottom-line results.

Resilience is not about hanging on doggedly to the past; rather, it's about challenging and often disrupting the status quo. Often the most seemingly difficult situations are actually windows of opportunity in disguise. When you sense your team closing down its options due to obstacles and barriers, help them refocus on what they want, rather than what they don't want.

As parents, teachers, managers, coaches, and leaders, we need to remember that we do not control other people; we only affect them through our vision, actions, words, and examples.

We can't open the WOOs for them; we can only let them know they are right there. The only person we directly control is the one we see in the mirror. By becoming dedicated blame-busters, we become examples of character, responsibility, and maturity that will make a lasting difference as we travel together along the high road.

A WOO for You

For the next week, try on for size a new belief about communication, one that I have found is a surefire way to develop the habit of blame busting. The belief statement is: "The meaning of my communication is the response I generate." As this belief takes hold in your spirit, you will take new responsibility for your communication. If someone doesn't seem to understand you or appears to have latched onto a meaning you didn't intend, rather than blaming them, seek to change yourself. Keep trying new ways to express yourself until it works. With a fresh new belief, you'll find yourself traveling the high road. And the view will amaze you.

10

Networking That Works!

For many years I felt very uncomfortable and nervous at the thought of cocktail parties, business socials, or events where I would be thrown into a room of people I didn't know. It was so far out of my comfort zone I created reasons to avoid such occasions. If I couldn't find a way out, I would devise a way to slip out as quickly as I could. I saw these not as windows of opportunity but as windows to jump out of so that I could run away.

Yet deep down I knew that one of the most important skills to develop in business and life today is networking. Our ability to easily connect with people and build meaningful relationships swiftly can do more to generate tremendously significant WOOs than perhaps any other proficiency we can develop. I am eternally grateful to my great friend John Locke for helping me see networking with completely different eyes.

John is the best networker I know. Everyone seems to know and admire him because he exemplifies the four secrets to the power of relationships: seek to give rather than get; ask more than tell; be a passionate presence; and follow up beyond expectation.

When John meets people, he is genuinely interested in them. People love that. He is full of questions and keenly observant about what's important to them. He truly wants to hear their answers, and then he actually listens before he formulates his responses, one of the most powerful relationship skills there is. He taught me to remember that we have two eyes, two ears, and only one mouth—and how important it is to maintain that ratio in our interactions.

John is looking not for what he can get from another person but for what he can give. As he listens he looks for connections that will serve that individual. He *asks* and only rarely *tells*. He instantly creates trust with the other person because we can sense that his wheels are turning to discover WOOs for us. He clearly seeks to serve, and service is love in action. He is excited about building connections for others without thinking about what it will bring him. And there is a natural law he puts into effect through this authentic desire to serve: "Whenever we seek to enrich another's experience, we can't help but enrich our own."

What happens when we apply John's networking principles? When we ask more than tell it becomes much easier to be fully present, because we're not caught up in worrying about what we're going to say next. It is a difference—even a dramatic shift—that is palpable to the person with whom we are talking. By seeking first to serve and understand rather than seeking to be understood, we build great rapport and trust. We help others feel important and interesting. The other magical benefit of this kind of extraordinary networking is that for people like me, who have long felt uncomfortable in networking situations, it puts us at ease. It takes the pressure off and moves us from ego to *we*-go.

But John goes a step further. He is what I call *passionately* present. When you are speaking with John, you feel as though you are the most important person on the planet. Have you ever been around people who make you feel extraordinarily special and appreciated? How do they *do* this? This extraordinary level of presence is born from John's deep fascination with other people. He loves to listen to others' stories because of his belief that there is something remarkable, unique, and impressive about every individual. This belief, combined with his passion to serve, leaves those he talks to with the unmistakable sense that he truly cares about us.

It is John's uncanny follow-up, however, that truly cements his place as the best networker I know. Because he has been so fully present with us, he remembers key elements of our conversations. He internalizes what is important to us, key details we discussed, and ways he can serve us. So when he follows up with a phone call, a face-to-face meeting, a text, or an email, he injects those very personal and significant points into his communication. We appreciate how remarkably well he listened; this is a man who walks his talk when it comes to following through on promises and commitments.

When we seek to give rather than get, ask more than tell, are passionately present, and follow up beyond expectation, what do you think happens to the way we view "networking"? Guided by these simple principles, we relish the opportunity to meet new people and learn how we can serve them. We build trust and respect naturally, through our authentic love of giving. And others will want to reciprocate because we have shown them that we feel they truly matter. The results are dynamic WOOs not just for us but for everyone we touch.

A WOO for You

Over the course of the week, as you meet new people, focus on John's four secrets to networking:

1. Seek to give rather than get.
2. Ask more than tell.
3. Be a passionate presence.
4. Follow up beyond expectation.

If you tend to be introspective and retiring when meeting new people, these four secrets might help you relax and feel much more comfortable. And if you are already outgoing and extroverted, these secrets may serve to remind you about John's magic ratio: that you have two eyes and two ears but only one mouth. Use them in that proportion, and every opportunity to establish new relationships with others just might become a dynamic WOO for everyone you meet.

11

The Superglue That Binds Us Together

I have a secret to share, one that has rarely been taught. It involves a tool every one of us can use to help others see themselves with fresh eyes. This powerful tool is like superglue; it sticks with us forever. It can amaze, delight, and elevate our spirit. This magical tool is called *surprise*.

The Canadian airline WestJet has built the power and magic of surprise into the heart of their culture. During the holiday season, when air travel can be especially daunting and tiresome, hundreds of WestJet employees volunteered thousands of hours to create some magical holiday surprises for their passengers.

Using some state-of-the art technology, they set up a full-length video screen in the Toronto airport from which Santa greeted each family boarding flights traveling on Christmas Eve from Toronto to Hamilton and Calgary. The looks of wonder and amazement were unforgettable as Santa spoke to every parent and child by name and asked what they wanted for Christmas, as if he were not on a video screen but rather right there with them. Of course, through the magic of technology he *was* able to see and hear them, so he could playfully interact with them about their reactions and expressions. Both the parents and the children were completely smitten.

As the passengers talked with Santa, hidden WestJet volunteers wrote down what they said they wanted for Christmas. In a flash the lists were scanned and sent to Hamilton and Calgary, where more WestJetters were primed and ready to zip all over town to purchase the gifts the passengers had told Santa they most wanted. They rushed these gifts back to the airports in Calgary and Hamilton, where still more volunteers wrapped them, placed large gift tags on each present, and hustled them to the luggage crew.

When the buzzer went off and the luggage carousels sprang into motion, the travelers stood in astonishment as these beautifully wrapped personalized gifts floated down to them one by one. At that moment Santa appeared, this time in person, giving a jolly "ho-ho-ho" and spreading holiday cheer. The tears, laughter, and pure joy on the faces of the children in that baggage claim created a moment of joy that none present would ever forget.

WestJet's "Christmas Miracles" were captured on video thanks to dozens of hidden cameras. The edited YouTube video generated hundreds of thousands of views and a level of positive public relations rarely ever received by a company in any industry. The effect on the WestJet employees is no less remarkable and valuable. By drawing on the impact of surprise, WestJet team members felt a heightened sense of pride and commitment to their company. They realize that they are a part of something very special.

When we seize the WOO to deliver meaningful surprises for people who are important in our lives, we create fresh possibilities for dynamic change. Perhaps the most memorable surprise I've helped to coordinate was my wife's fiftieth-birthday surprise. It turned out to be an event that radiates with transformational power to this day.

When I think of my wife, I know I am the luckiest man on the face of the earth. Carole is my greatest teacher, my best friend, and the love of my life. So when the big milestone of her fiftieth birthday came into view, I wanted to create a moment of surprise for Carole she would never forget—a moment that would express far more eloquently than words how deeply she is loved and appreciated. I wanted Carole to experience a moment that would lift her whenever she encountered disappointment, self-doubt, or stress in the future.

It was with this compelling vision that the seed of Carole's birthday was planted nearly a year before.

In January, as I flew to New York City for a speaking engagement, I chanced upon an article about the Broadway stage version of Disney's *The Lion King*. And it struck me that a fantastic gift would be to fly all four members of our family to the Big Apple to celebrate her fiftieth by attending the show. It would be fun not just for her but also for our daughters, Kelsey and Jenna; I looked forward to all four of us tasting the Big Apple together. But as I began to think about the planning needed to pull off this surprise, I began to think more deeply about Carole and what was truly most important to her in her life.

It was then that the light bulb went off. Carole's greatest passion is for her friends and family. New York was electric, Broadway exciting, but without sharing her fiftieth with the people she loves so dearly, it would be just another birthday and another trip. All at once I knew that the heart and soul of Carole's celebration would be a totally different surprise than I had originally envisioned. We would still fly to New York City for her birthday weekend. We would still go see *The Lion King*. But when we arrived in the city, she would be met somewhere totally unexpectedly by the friends and family who have filled her life with love. All at once I knew the reason I had accumulated my zillion frequent flyer miles as a professional speaker. It was for Carole.

I waited for more than an hour outside the ticket office at the theater. When I finally made it to the window, there was no block of four seats available for *The Lion King* until March of the following year—five months after Carole's birthday—*except* for the Sunday matinee on November 12, the very weekend I had planned. I snatched up those seats in a flash, high-fiving the people behind me as I left the box office in triumph.

As those close to me know all too well, I've been known to get so excited about surprises that I've occasionally spilled the beans in advance of the event. So I decided to devise a decoy plan to throw Carole completely off track. I figured the best way to keep such an enormous surprise from my clever wife was to let her think she already knew it.

So when I arrived home from New York City I "accidentally" left the *Lion King* tickets out where I knew she'd run across them. When she found them and pressed me for an explanation, I crumbled. With feigned exasperation I carried on about what an ignoramus I was to have left the tickets out. "At least we can still surprise Kelsey and Jenna," I moaned.

Carole bought the act lock, stock, and barrel. After all, it was so like me to botch the surprise. Now she was my partner in crime, completely desensitized to anything but keeping the plan from our daughters.

During the months leading up to her birthday, I set to

work arranging for Carole's closest lifetime friends to meet us in New York City. As I began making calls, I was completely awed by the response of Carole's friends to the plan. Without hesitation, every one of them jumped in with unfettered enthusiasm. Our wonderful friends Robert and Kristie were the most amazing of all. They were the only participants who lived in the New York City area—on Long Island, in the lovely little haven of Sea Cliff. Though I was able to use frequent flyer miles for many of the guests, the cost of flying in so many people was pretty steep, so I asked if some of those coming in could stay with the Werz family at their home. Their answer stunned me: "No, *some* of the guests will not do. *All* of your friends are welcome at our home. We don't have tons of space, but it will be fun."

These remarkable people opened their hearts and their home to seventeen travelers, most of whom they had never met. The common bond was the love they all shared for Carole— and that was more than enough.

We were to fly to New York on Saturday; as the whole plan developed, it became clear that I needed to get everyone else there on Friday because of varying travel schedules. They would occupy virtually every square foot of floor space at the Werzes' with sleeping bags and blankets—a grown-up slumber party.

With travel plans set, I turned my attention to the surprise party itself. Carole adores East Indian cuisine, and thanks to some extraordinary help from Kristie I was able to find the perfect restaurant, the Bukhara Grill. I explained the whole plan to Raja, the restaurant manager, and he enthusiastically promised to take great care of us. The vision was becoming more of a reality by the minute.

One of Carole's closest friends, Muff, had a history of orchestrating special parties for friends' birthdays and anniversaries. These fantasy events included a *Great Gatsby* gala, a 1960s-style senior prom à la the Broadway show *Grease*, and an Ethiopian tribal celebration. The formula for these events always included costumes and full-out role-playing. Carole had participated in many of these parties during the years she and Muff were housemates in Alaska. In fact, she had co-planned many of the events, and she treasured those memories.

Carole's fiftieth gave Muff the perfect opportunity to bring her fantasy experience skills out of storage with a group of people charged up with enthusiasm. This was to be no standard birthday party.

Everything was arranged for our friends to meet the four of us at the Bukhara Grill at four-thirty on Saturday afternoon. Carole knew only that we were arriving in Newark at two-thirty on Saturday and would surprise the girls by taking them to see *The Lion King* at one o'clock on Sunday afternoon.

On Friday we packed bags for the girls while they were at school. When they came home that afternoon, I told them I was going to take Mom shopping while they were at dance practice on Saturday morning. I added that we'd have to leave a little early Saturday to swing by the airport because one of my bags had been misrouted from my trip earlier that week and had finally come in. It was not at all unusual for my bags to arrive late, so both of the girls were oblivious to any trickery. Carole was thoroughly enjoying the entire thing.

Late Friday night, as Carole unwound in a hot bath, I snuck downstairs to check my email one last time before the big day. Sure enough, there was a message from Kristie posted less than a half hour before. The message practically jumped off the screen. Kristie relayed how much fun everyone was having together making plans, and that they had come up with something terrific.

I was to tell Carole that I had been surfing the Net for cool things to do in New York City and had found something she'd really enjoy. It was the hottest thing in the Big Apple—a new traveling dinner theater group called the Way-Off Broadway Players. They would be performing at a five-star Indian restaurant, the Bukhara Grill, on Saturday evening. We needed to arrive by four-thirty because the first show would begin shortly thereafter and the second show was already sold out. Kristie ended the email by telling me this was going to be better than anyone could have imagined. I didn't know what they were up to, but with that kind of synergy and exuberance, I couldn't wait to find out.

Carole and I had to turn our heads away to hide our grins when the girls glided downstairs ready for dance practice Saturday morning wearing their fluffy blue slippers. They were going to be quite the sensation on the plane! We gobbled down a quick breakfast and jumped in the van (we had loaded the luggage the night before while the girls were asleep).

When we arrived at the airport, I said: "Why don't you all go in and pick out something at the snack bar to eat after dance?" The girls, in their typical Saturday morning daze, strolled off into the terminal, fluffy slippers and all.

I took the van to the parking lot and scampered back with our luggage to check in. The girls walked by after using the restroom but didn't see me in line.

"The bag is up at the gate. We need to go up there," I reported matter-of-factly. Like good soldiers, Kelsey and Jenna dutifully followed me up to the gate just as the flight was beginning to board. It wasn't until I handed our boarding cards to the gate agent and started walking down the jetway that it finally occurred to Kelsey that something odd was going on.

"Are we getting on this plane?" she asked with a look of bewilderment on her face.

Once at our seats the girls determinedly tried to get us to tell them where we were going. "Are we going to Charlotte to go shopping? Are we going to Disney World? Please tell us!" But we were having too much fun. The mystery remained unsolved for the girls when we arrived in Charlotte and made our way to the connecting gate. They saw that our next flight was to Newark, but they didn't have a clue where that was! Carole and I couldn't stop smiling.

When we were about an hour away from Newark, I casually leaned over and told Carole about the reservations I had made for the dinner show featuring the "Way-Off-Broadway Players." I said I had found out about it on the Internet and it looked like fun. She was enthusiastic about the idea and clearly didn't suspect any surprise.

After landing in Newark and dealing with our bags, we hailed a taxi for the heart of the city. Everyone was excited by the sight of the Statue of Liberty and the mammoth Empire State Building. None of the girls had any idea where we were staying until the cab pulled to a stop in front of the Palace Hotel. My three ladies felt like royalty as we made our way up to our room on the twenty-sixth floor. Our view looked straight down on venerable St. Patrick's Cathedral, with dozens of New York's classic skyscrapers touching the sky all around us.

We had only enough time to clean up a bit before heading out to the Bukhara Grill. I had made the reservation at the Palace six months before finding the restaurant, and had no idea the two were located only two blocks away from each other. No cab necessary, we left the hotel at 4:25 and strolled leisurely over to the restaurant. In fact, I had to stall a bit along the way so we wouldn't arrive early.

When we reached the restaurant I held the door open, not so much out of chivalry but because I wanted to be positioned behind Carole and the girls so that my pounding heart and rising excitement wouldn't give anything away. As soon as they stepped inside they were met by a man and woman dressed elegantly and wearing brightly colored ceramic masks. They bowed formally, handed us all playbills describing the Way-Off-Broadway Players, and escorted us upstairs, past the main dining area. Kelsey and Jenna looked a little apprehensive as they climbed the stairs because the escorts did not speak, but rather gestured and guided us through mime. Carole, on the other hand, seemed quite swept up in the spirit of the festivity, ready to play and interact with the actors as the playbill instructed.

After what seemed like an eternity to me (though it was only a few seconds), we entered the banquet room. It was a sight to behold. A beautifully decorated grand dining table stretched before us while all around the most bizarre looking group of "performers" we'd ever seen danced and spun around the room. Each wore a flamboyant costume with an even wilder mask. None of the actors spoke to us, though they hummed and whistled to tunes of their own creation. They immediately pulled us into their midst and attempted to get us to join them in their contortions. Carole clearly thought this was a little odd but fun, and she went along with them. The girls, however, tightened up with discomfort and fired one of those looks at me that said, *Dad, what have you gotten us into this time?*

After a few moments of this strange activity, the players

gestured to us to sit down at the head of the table. We did as instructed and then watched in mild surprise as the actors also sat down around the table. Carole spoke up playfully: "Look, isn't this neat? The performers are going to eat with us." Judging by the looks on the girls' faces, I'm pretty certain at this point they would have hit the exit at a dead run if it had been up to them.

Once everyone was seated, Carole was handed a little note that read,

For the Lady . . .
The Way-Off-Broadway Players welcome you to the show.
Kindly ask one of the players to remove their mask. When
you are ready to continue on, proceed to the next player of
your choice.

I held my breath and watched as Carole turned to one of the actors wearing a costume reminiscent of a medieval queen's and invited her to unveil herself. Ever so slowly the actor lifted her mask. Carole let out a shriek of surprise and delight. "Oh my God! Margie!" I glanced quickly at Kelsey and Jenna. Instantly their trepidation was replaced with sheer amazement. Carole seemed to be laughing and crying all at once. Then she asked the man standing beside Margie to remove his mask because she could now recognize from his tall and slender build that he had to be Margie's husband, Tad. Carole rushed over to our dear friends from our years in Montana and embraced them joyously. The best part was that when Carole saw Margie and Tad, she assumed that they had driven in from Wisconsin for her birthday—but that all the others in the room were actors. She still had no idea that the entire cast of the Way-Off-Broadway Players were not players at all.

As Carole stood arm in arm with Margie and Tad, she was reminded that she was to choose other players to reveal themselves. Looking across the table, she pointed to the man and woman wearing the ceramic tragedy masks who had escorted us up to the banquet room. Carole's voice shot up an octave in astonishment as Muff and her husband, Zig, emerged from behind their masks.

I choked up with emotion when I saw Muff's reaction. Muff is one of the most wonderful people I know. Caring, compassionate, fun, and spirited, Muff has been a spiritual sister to Carole. Their connection runs deep, as they lived together, found their husbands at just about the same time, and gave birth to their daughters two days apart. But through all the remarkable, magical times we had spent with Muff, I had never seen her out of control, swept away by her feelings—never until this moment. Her mouth opened, her eyes welled up, and she burst into tears. Carole ran over to her and they held each other with unrestrained affection.

One by one, Carole had the players reveal themselves. It was not until her sister, June, pulled off her Jesse Ventura mask (I didn't even know who she was under that hilarious disguise) that it finally hit Carole that all of the players were actually her friends and family. She had been so convinced that this was an off-Broadway show, and so completely unsuspecting that anything like this could be happening, that as each mask came off, her surprise heightened.

These special people did so much more than show up. They all wrote letters to Carole expressing their love and describing how she had touched their lives. They brought with them a mirror encircled by a golden wreath and each gave her a little memento to hang from it that symbolized the unique and precious relationships they shared with Carole. One by one they came to the head of the table, embraced her, read their notes of love, and explained the meaning of their gifts.

I stood holding the mirror as each of her cherished friends hung their gifts on the golden wreath. The woman I love more than life itself seemed to glow, as if she understood, for the first time, the difference she has made in the lives of the people she loves, simply by being herself. And just beyond her I saw our two daughters, looking at their mother being honored as few people ever are in their lifetime. They saw their mom, the person in their lives who never seeks credit or praise, receiving unconditional love from everyone in the room. It was the best moment of my life.

When we returned to the hotel late that night Carole pulled me aside and gently took my hand. Her eyes were wet with tears as she said with great conviction, "My life will never be the same. If I ever begin to lose faith in myself or think that I don't really matter, I'll remember this night."

The real magic of the surprise was in its power to transform. Ignited by her birthday surprise and the realization that she was significant in so many lives, Carole created breakthrough after breakthrough in the weeks, months, and years that followed. Tackling her fear of speaking in public, she joined Toastmasters and soon was delivering presentations at meetings every week. She was elected the president of the Parent Association of our girls' school, where she led meetings and developed her leadership skills. After three years of intensive study she became a licensed spiritual practitioner at her church, where she continues to help others overcome their fears and doubts.

This is the power of surprise. In creating surprises, we enable others to see WOOs they otherwise would have missed.

They see themselves with fresh eyes. And when we change the way we see ourselves, the self we see will change. It doesn't get any better than that.

A WOO for You

What if you planned and delivered surprises for one or two important people in your life within the next six months? These could be for family members, colleagues at work, or even customers. The surprises need not be anywhere near as extravagant as Carole's. It could be as simple as a heartfelt handwritten card sent just for the heck of it, rather than to commemorate a birthday, anniversary, or formal occasion. In fact, the unexpected timing can add power to your surprise. Just be sure the surprise is focused on them rather than yourself. When you dive into planning these surprises, you will be amazed at the WOOs that suddenly appear for everyone involved.

12

The Most Precious Present

What is the most important gift we can provide to our loved ones, our teammates, our friends, and our customers that truly lets them know that they are significant to us? In both our personal and professional relationships nothing is more important to building trust and connection than being fully present. When we are fully present, 100 percent of our mind, body, and spirit are with the people we are with *now*. There are no WOOs lying in wait in the past. They exist only in the present. And they are the keys to an extraordinary future.

Yet has it ever been more challenging to be fully present? We are so swept up in our busy-ness and our technology that genuine presence is too often choked out of our days. According to the *Huffington Post*, we now spend an average of nine and a half hours of our time awake each day on non-voice mobile digital devices and watching television. In contrast, the average American father spends seven to eight hours *a week* in actual interaction with his children, according to the Pew Research Institute. Spending as much time as I do on airplanes and in airports, I am struck by how rare it is to find people conversing, laughing, and enjoying one another these days. We're all on our phones, watching movies on our entertainment consoles aboard the plane, or zoning out on our musical playlists. I sometimes chuckle to myself when I see a couple who have gone out to a restaurant to spend quality time together on their cell phones, completely immersed in Facebook, checking scores on ESPN, or texting madly. We're conditioning ourselves to not be present, missing out on the magnificent gift that only true presence provides.

Ralph Waldo Emerson said, "What you do screams so loudly that I cannot hear what you say." When it comes to making someone feel like they matter, presence speaks louder than words. Presence sends an unmistakable message to others, telling them that they are important and valued. The message is genuine, too, because we simply can't *fake* being present. Don't we know instantly when others are really there or when their minds are in another area code? And it's not enough to simply be physically present—true presence also requires focused attention and engagement. All this is becoming increasingly rare. The explosion of personal technology is creating a huge challenge to being present as we spend more time playing with apps than talking and connecting with one another.

When my daughters were both little girls they managed to break through my thick skull to teach me that the most precious gift I could ever give others is presence. We moved to Montana when Kelsey was eight and Jenna was almost three, and settled in the little town of Hamilton to escape the rush and pressure of the big city. We felt that small-town life would give us more time together, more opportunity to be fully present for each other as a family as the girls were growing up. It was an exciting time for me professionally because my speaking business was blooming and I had a huge consulting contract for a fast-growing direct-sales company, helping them with their marketing, communication, and training. To top it all off, I had just finished writing my first book and was immersed in the promotional campaign to build sales momentum for it.

It's almost hard to believe now because we are so accustomed to today's technology, but in those days email, text, and social media had not yet caught fire, so the main tool for communication was still the phone. My office was upstairs in our wonderful old Victorian home, next to the bedroom Kelsey and Jenna shared.

Because I was dealing with many time zones, I started my day very early, jumping on the phone for my consulting work or doing radio interviews for East Coast stations. I heard the girls wake up, but most days just gave them a quick good morning hug while Carole got them ready for school. When they came home in the afternoon I was still buzzing away in my office making call after call. They'd pop in and cuddle for a minute or two and then happily go off to do homework, dance, or play. I was so caught up in my work that the next thing I knew it was time to get them ready for bed. Every night my plan was to come to their room to spend time with them reading stories, tickling, and laughing before they went to sleep. Just the thought of those moments with my sweet girls made me grin.

But every night as I headed to their room to tuck them in, I walked right by my office. And there, directly in my line of sight was that darn telephone. I knew that in the short time I had spent downstairs getting a bite to eat or helping clean up, I would have accumulated at least a dozen new voicemails. So while Kelsey and Jenna brushed their teeth and put on their pajamas, I detoured into my office—for just a few minutes—to knock off some of those nagging voicemails. I wouldn't be long. One quick call, then I'd be back with my girls to be the dad I wanted to be.

Well I'll bet you can guess what happened. Two hours later I'd finally hang up the phone. Carole had tucked the girls in and read them bedtime stories. She'd cuddled and loved them while I plowed through my calls. Hours later I'd walk over to their room, now dark and quiet, and tiptoe to their bedside. Though they didn't know it, I'd give each a kiss and stand there for a moment looking at the most beautiful little girls on the earth. Then I'd slip out, silently promising myself that tomorrow would be different. Tomorrow I would be there and make sure they knew how much I loved them. Tomorrow I would be present.

But the next day that darn phone was still there. This pattern went on for days that rolled into weeks that turned into months. Finally Kelsey and Jenna decided to teach their daddy a lesson he would never forget.

One night, just as I had settled into my chair ready to pick up the phone, I felt two shining lights in my office door. I truly *felt* their presence. The energy was radiant. When I turned to look, both girls ran to me. The next thing I knew Jenna had nosed her way up into my lap like a golden retriever positioning for a good ear scratch. And Kelsey had her arm around me, looking up with those incredibly sweet eyes of hers. I was surprised and delighted and couldn't help but smile as I lapped up their affection. I asked, "What's all this about?"

Kelsey, as the senior sister and therefore the official spokeswoman, took charge. With both girls looking right through me into my heart, she asked, "Daddy, before we go to sleep we just wanted to ask you something."

I replied, "Sure. What is it?"

"Daddy, we just wanted to know, do you love your phone more than you love us?"

It was as if someone had taken a sword and plunged it through my heart. I could barely breathe. Though I hugged them tightly and reassured them how much I loved them, deep down inside I realized that my actions and decisions had been teaching my daughters that they weren't as important as my telephone. The realization shook me to my soul.

It was I who tucked them in that night. And I never missed another goodnight WOO unless I was away on a speaking trip. From that day forward my calendar started and ended with my family. If the girls had a dance recital, an awards program at school, or any event that mattered to them, it was blocked off and off-limits for anything else. I was the one to get them ready for school and often to pick them up and take them to dance practice. And I thought I was doing this for them.

Though I had no idea at the time, every single dimension of our lives was elevated by the simple decision to be more fully present. By living by that decision through conscious focus and committed action, I found that I became far more productive and balanced.

When we are fully present more consistently in our lives, the same will be true for all of us. Do you know that the real secret to life balance is not time? It is being present—because five minutes of full presence with someone we love is worth five years of faking it. And every time we are fully present our actions say to that special person, "You are important. You are significant. You matter and you count."

A wonderful little poem brings the vision of full presence into perfect focus.

The past is history . . .
The future, a mystery . . .
The gift is now!
That's why we call it the present.

When we are present for WOOs that are a bit outside our comfort zones, we may just find hidden treasures we never dreamed existed. I experienced such a moment when Carole and I drove up to meet Kelsey and Jenna in Washington, D.C., for an once-in-a-lifetime event that was definitely not up my alley. We were coming together to buy Kelsey her wedding dress.

When it comes to my list of desired activities, a day of shopping falls between "cleaning the rain gutters" and "root canal." Add in the emotional whammy of prepping myself to walk my daughter down the aisle and I was toast. The very thought of this trip made me want to find a chair, sit down, and stay put. *I know as much about wedding dresses as I do about nuclear physics,* I thought. *I'll just be dead weight.* My initial impulse was to pass on the day and I figured that Kelsey had asked me just to be kind, that no one really wanted me there.

I called Kelsey a week or two before the big weekend and tried to make it easy for her to tell me it really didn't matter to her if I came. But to my surprise she truly wanted me to be a part of the day. It really mattered to her. I love Kelsey more than I can ever adequately express, so if it meant something to her, I didn't need to hear any more. Despite the fact that my sense of style is really more of an affliction, I was in. Not only that, I was determined to elevate my energy for the day.

To my astonishment, by five o'clock that Saturday afternoon I had experienced one of the best days of my life. All day long at three very different wedding dress boutiques I had sat and watched as my gorgeous daughter tried on dozens of lovely wedding dresses. She was absolutely radiant and glowing. She took my breath away.

Throughout the day Carole, Jenna, and Kelsey's best friend, Maggie, all offered insightful observations to help Kelsey with her decision. All I did was grin and kept stammering, "You are so beautiful." A couple of times I ventured out with tentative comments like "That's really slimming" or "I love the bow in the back," and everyone humored me by pretending there was actual value in what I had to say. But I knew better. I was a complete ignoramus about style, fit, and look. But I didn't care. All that mattered to me were the indelible portraits that were being permanently framed in my heart as I watched my little girl who had grown into such an amazing woman try on dress after dress.

As the day ended, one of those pictures stood above all the rest. In the moment that Kelsey decided on *the* dress and we all said, "It's yours," I saw a happiness radiate through her entire being that I have wanted her to experience since the day she was born. Joy flew from her and wrapped us all in its glow as Kelsey announced, "I'm really getting married!"

Since that wonderful day I've tried to figure out why she actually wanted me there with her. And I think I know. *Presence.* I think the reason Kelsey wanted her goofball dad there to share her day was that after that fateful day in Hamilton, Montana, when my daughters woke me up to the importance of being present, I'd never missed the other moments that mattered to her as she was growing up. I went to every dance performance, every school assembly and awards program, every parade, every college scouting trip. I was there to help her find her high school graduation dress and was just as inept then as I am now. But here's the key: I didn't just show up at these events—*I loved them.* I was there because I loved her. I was fully present, and that communicated beyond words to her how important she is to me. That's what the people that we care about need to know—that they are significant, that they truly matter, and that they are important.

No one ever told me this when my girls were small. I just lucked into it. But no matter what we've done before, we can get this one right now. We can be there, be present, and enjoy every precious moment. Though we may think we're doing it for others, the happiness and fulfillment will come back to us tenfold.

When we apply the principle of being fully present in our professional lives, we build the same kind of trust and connection as in our personal relationships. By being fully present with our customers, teammates, vendors, and colleagues, we fill them with the sense that they are truly valued and appreciated.

One of the great gifts of my life was the WOO I experienced to become the friend of the greatest men's college basketball coach of all time. John Wooden led UCLA to ten national championships in the final twelve years of his career. No other men's college basketball coach had won as many as five until Coach Mike Krzyzewski, "Coach K," guided Duke to their fifth title in 2015. But as great as John Wooden was as a coach, he was an even better husband, father, and human being.

Coach Wooden exemplified many of the finest leadership qualities, including integrity, wisdom, kindness, and humility. But perhaps his greatest gift was his presence. When you were in his company he made you feel as if you were the most important person in the world. When he was with you, 100 percent of his mind and spirit were completely focused on your interaction, whether you were a star player, an assistant coach, or a young man who called out of the blue without introduction and asked to interview him. The inevitable outcome of spending even a short time with Coach Wooden was that you left feeling a little better about yourself. He lifted everyone he touched through his authenticity and presence.

Another person who exhibits an amazing sense of presence is legendary speaker and business leader Dr. Nido Qubein. Dr. Qubein has mastered the art of using technology to deliver a remarkable level of presence that surprises and delights everyone connected to him.

Dr. Qubein came to the United States as a young man from the Middle East in 1966 knowing not a word of English and with about $50 to his name. Though his pockets were empty, his spirit was overflowing with enthusiasm, determination, and an insatiable hunger to learn and grow. His real language in the early years of his new life in America was his full presence, through which he communicated his desire to serve and to work hard to provide value in everything he did. It was in these early years that Nido discovered a secret that would serve him extraordinarily well over the course of a remarkable career. He would be quicker and more enthusiastic to respond to opportunities than anyone expected and in so doing, he would build greater trust and stronger relationships with everyone he met. He would seize WOOs rather than wait for them.

That focus has propelled Dr. Qubein to tremendous success personally and professionally. As the president of High Point University, he has led the school to unprecedented national prominence academically and financially. The city of High Point, North Carolina, had been devastated by recession and the downturn of the furniture manufacturing business that had been the lifeblood of the area. High Point University has injected fresh vitality and opportunity that has helped significantly to rebuild the local economy. He has been the chairman of the Great Harvest Bread Company and serves on the boards of directors for such leading companies as La-Z-Boy Corporation and BB&T. Dr. Qubein is also one of the most highly decorated and sought-after professional speakers in the world.

Through it all, Dr. Qubein has never forgotten the value of full presence and of responding more swiftly than anyone expects. Despite the enormous demands upon his time from his roles as university president, business executive, and professional speaker, he simply astonishes everyone with whom he interacts by responding to emails and texts more rapidly than they can believe, nearly always within one hour or less. I call it technological presence.

When I reached out to Dr. Qubein to bring him to my community of Asheville, North Carolina, to be our featured speaker at a major event that benefitted various local charities, I experienced firsthand his remarkable presence. He responded within minutes to every one of the fifteen emails or texts I sent him. And though his replies were short and crisp, they were personal, thoughtful, and focused. I came away from my communications with Dr. Qubein in awe of his amazing responsiveness and with the feeling that he genuinely cared about me and our community. He helped me see that we express full presence even through the very technology that I had so often seen as a hindrance to meaningful connection and relationship.

A WOO for You

How can you break the habit of not being present? How can you begin to strengthen the practice of presence in your life?

Choose one person at home and one at work to whom you wish to be more present for the next thirty days. This doesn't mean you must spend more time with them. Indeed, your schedule may mean you have less time with them. But what would happen if when you're with them you put away your cell phone? What if you listened fully to what they have to say rather than thinking about what you're going to say next? What if you asked a few more questions and turned up your level of alertness to what they're communicating beyond just words? After just a few days, I believe you will sense a closer connection and enhanced energy between the two of you. They may even begin to look at you differently. You will be on your way to strengthening the extraordinary power of presence in your relationship with them.

13

Just Listen!

For many of us, one of the biggest challenges in our personal and professional lives is dealing with the people we're pretty certain God put on the planet to bug us. In fact, one of the biggest reasons we leave a position in an organization to find another is because there is someone we must interact with regularly with whom we simply can't seem to get along.

We all have people whom we feel so connected with it's as if we're telepathic. On the phone we say the same thing at the same moment and laugh at our synchronicity. We seem to know exactly what the other is thinking and embrace every opportunity to work together, converse, or even just hang out. It's so *easy* with them.

Yet we have those other people in our lives that test us (and our patience). Instead of great synchronicity, we feel as though they are the rocks to our windows. But isn't it interesting that sometimes our biggest tests are people who matter most to us? Sometimes it's our spouse, our partner, our son or daughter, or someone essential on our own team, and we know that if we can't find a way to make it mesh, we can't possibly win. Deep down inside we know that if they were ever really in trouble, we'd run through fire for them, but over time, because of different perspectives, we may have become abrasive. We've forgotten how powerful we are when we get back to being *embracive*. And finding that power starts with listening.

When I became the vice president of a large training company in San Diego, our head of customer service felt a great deal of resentment toward me because she had been intensely loyal to my predecessor and thought that I had somehow been the cause of his departure. Though this was not the case, her iciness toward me and my ineffectiveness in finding a way to ease the tension between us was affecting our whole team. Everyone seemed to tiptoe around the office as if it were a minefield, terrified an explosion might occur at any moment. We were falling behind on deadlines and not fulfilling our promises to our customers.

Finally one day I asked her to come into my office. Once she sat down I said, "You are so important to this team and I *know* we can find a way to work together so much more effectively. So for ten minutes, if you will allow me, I will just listen to you. You are free to say whatever is on your mind, and I promise I won't interrupt or defend. I'll just listen. After your ten minutes, I'll ask if you would just listen to me for ten."

I'll never forget her response. Looking quite skeptical, she said, "I don't think I can talk for ten minutes."

I simply asked, "Would you try?"

An hour later she stopped talking! I kept my promise and didn't say a word. I just listened. In fact, I didn't even get my ten minutes! But from that moment on our relationship transformed, as we treated each other with new respect and genuine eagerness to work together. We accomplished more over the next year—and had more fun doing it—than I would have dreamed possible. Today, more than twenty years later, our friendship continues.

Perhaps the greatest of all human needs is the need to feel heard. When we listen to others without focusing on what we're going to say next, we communicate to others that we truly value them. This genuine listening is a real secret to being fully present. We build their trust at the core level. They, in turn, are much more interested in listening to what we have to say. By listening, we break through and connect with others far better than we could by trying to convince them to come over to our side. We empower rather than overpower. Taking time to just listen is a surprising and tremendously enriching WOO.

A WOO for You

Is there someone on your team with whom you find it increasingly difficult to get along? Why not set up a just-listen session? It's important that you arrange the meeting in advance and have it away from distractions and the normal stress of the day so that neither of you feels rushed or pressured when you sit down to talk. You can set the stage for your just-listen session by honestly expressing your desire to build a stronger relationship that creates a win-win for both of you. And remember, once they begin, they can talk about whatever is on their mind. Always let them speak first, and stick to your promise to just listen—no defending, correcting, or responding in any way other than full presence. Listen as though the next words they say may change both of your lives for the better.

Just-listen sessions can be just as important at home with the people you love the most. At least once or twice a year my wife, Carole, and I arrange a just-listen date. It's so easy in the rush and gush of daily life to drift into autopilot mode and stop really listening to each other. We always feel refreshed and reconnected after these little sessions. Try it—you may, too!

14

Giver and Receiver

Let me ask a few important questions about giving and receiving. How many of us find it much more comfortable to give a compliment than to receive one? How many of us squirm away from compliments quickly, thinking something like, *If you'd seen me this morning, you wouldn't be saying that*? How many of us feel that if we allow ourselves to enjoy a compliment, we are not being humble or modest?

Conversely, how do we feel inside when we give to others? Isn't it one of the best feelings of all?

When we really think about it, what is receiving? Receiving is allowing others to feel the joy of giving. And when we receive poorly, we snatch that feeling of joy away.

So if we truly want to help others become generous, if we want them to feel the joy of giving that we ourselves love so much, we must be open to a WOO most of us have never been taught: learning to receive.

In the last year of my coaching career, my senior swimmers plotted a special birthday surprise for me. They each wrote me personal cards and hid them with a big cake and other goodies in the weight room.

About halfway through practice that evening, Joe, one of my top swimmers, called out: "Coach, can we have relays tonight?"

I responded, "If you all work extra hard on this next set, we'll end practice with fifteen minutes of relays."

Little did I know that Joe's question was actually a secret signal to all the kids, because as soon as I set them off on the drill, they all sped to the end of the pool and climbed out. I had a mutiny on my hands!

Deep down inside I knew that this extraordinary behavior had something to do with my birthday. But at that time in my life I couldn't receive. I didn't understand what it meant. I was not a leader. I was a martyr.

So before they could get to the locker room and spring their surprise, I exploded at them.

"What do you think you're doing? Is this the kind of discipline we have on this team? This is just some excuse to get out of practice, isn't it?"

I'm not proud of my behavior that day. Five seconds before, the kids could have touched the sky. Now they froze where they were, not knowing whether to run and hide in the locker room or jump back in the pool and pretend nothing had happened. As they stood there devastated I looked into the stricken faces of these kids I adored, many of them with tears in their eyes, and I was suddenly swallowed by remorse. In that moment I finally realized what I was taking away because I couldn't receive.

So we had the party. It really wasn't that much fun because I'd pretty well killed the atmosphere. But from that day on I was determined to receive every gift or compliment with a heartfelt "Thank you!" Never again would I take away anyone's joy of giving.

Have you ever considered how much your appreciation really means? From a leadership perspective, those two words, "thank you," are perhaps the most important words to voice when it comes to building people, relationships, and teams. Opportunities to express genuine gratitude are among the most impactful WOOs of all, because when teammates feel appreciated, they engage. They shoot up from "Oh no!" to "Oh yeah!"

It is every bit as important for leaders to *receive* thanks graciously and genuinely as it is to give them. When you warmly receive others' thanks, you are teaching them that appreciation is not hierarchical but all-directional. The combination of giving and receiving gratitude creates organizations and families filled with personal responsibility and the belief that everyone is a leader and that everyone can make a difference. When we only give thanks but don't receive them well, we diminish others' belief that by bringing an attitude of gratitude to the team every single day they can lift everyone around them.

What's more, we will never be truly abundant until we learn to receive with real appreciation, because anytime abundance comes our way we will find ways to sabotage ourselves and push it away. If receiving poorly becomes a habit and our automatic response to compliments and gifts, we will build the disempowering belief within ourselves that we are not worthy of receiving. I know. I owned one of the largest swimming programs in the United States and I constantly struggled financially. It was only when I opened my heart to receiving and when I understood that my energy was my choice that I began a new path that has brought me real wealth: a family I adore, work I treasure, and the financial prosperity to live in a wonderful home, travel to incredible places, help others along the way, and enjoy every precious moment.

A WOO for You

What would it be like if when others give to you in any way—a smile, a kind word, a compliment, or a thoughtful gift—you received that gift with genuine joy and a heartfelt "Thank you"? You'll build a culture alive with giving, generosity, and unselfishness. One of the most surprising secrets to building these kinds of teams and relationships is the power of receiving, for when you receive with genuine appreciation you allow others to feel the joy of giving. Seize those WOOs to receive with honest appreciation.

DELIVERING BREAKTHROUGH RESULTS

15

Lighten Up, Don't Tighten Up .

When Mahatma Gandhi traveled across India preaching peace and nonviolence, a band of crazed fanatics rushed at his train, brandishing spears and clubs, determined to stop the gentle giant by force. Despite the desperate pleas of his aides and supporters, the Mahatma peacefully stepped out onto the train platform and smiled kindly as he looked into the shocked faces of the wild horde. Then, quite calmly but with just a hint of playfulness in his voice, he said, "You have every right to disagree with me—but must you also break my head?" His humor in the face of intense danger was so unexpected, so unnerving to the attackers, the effect was like a needle puncturing a balloon inflated to the limit. They stopped in their tracks, lowered their weapons, and quietly rode away. Gandhi understood the subtle power of humor and fun in the face of challenge.

Though we may not have thought about it a great deal before, how much is fun or the lack of it affecting us each day? What power does lightness of spirit and humor bring to the ongoing challenge called our busy lives, to our relationships, and to our performance?

The simple truth is, if we're not having fun in our work, we should probably try to do something else. If we're not having fun in our family, it will never be the family it could have been had there been a bit more laughter, a few more smiles, and a bit more fun. Most of all, if we're not having fun in the process of learning and growing, then learning won't have the adhesion and "stick" that learning is really all about. Learning is not so much about ideas as it is about *application* of ideas, because until we actually apply an idea it is simply words floating in the ethers. So when we sense that our teams or families are tightening up, maybe it's time to lighten up and have some fun!

In fact, one of the most powerful tools we can use to build relationships is a playful, surprising sense of humor, especially during times of stress and pressure. This can be difficult to remember, particularly in tough times. But you can turn the tide of negative emotion by lightening up, just as Gandhi deftly turned the mood of that frenzied mob.

How do we do it? How can we release some of the pressure that can often seem to build up like steam in a kettle? And what happens when we make a conscious effort to lighten up when others tighten up?

One of the easiest and most effective ways we can inject fun into our teams and families is by good-naturedly poking some fun at *ourselves*. We can lightheartedly joke about our own bungles and quirks rather than teasing others about theirs. As others see that we can laugh at ourselves, it becomes easier for them to lighten up about themselves.

Fear, anger, and frustration gather steam if unchecked. Humor is a magnificent pressure releaser. When we respond to challenges with wit and humor, we help others change their emotional state. They begin to look for the WOO instead of the woe.

But having fun is also a valuable and productive business goal. I have had the opportunity to speak to more than a thousand companies over the years. It is no coincidence that the company that jumps to my mind as having the most fun is also one of the great success stories in American business history, Southwest Airlines.

Southwest Airlines' culture revolves around three cornerstones: fun, love, and respect. They believe that when team members have fun and when they like coming to work, they are more productive and engaged. Time and time again Southwest has won the airline triple crown: best on-time performance, best baggage service, and fewest customer complaints. They have been rated as one of the three most admired American corporations. They carry more domestic travelers annually than any other American airline and now employ nearly fifty thousand people across the United States.

In my work with client companies both large and small, the best companies center their culture on clear and solid values. They work to instill these values into the hearts and minds of every team member. But Southwest Airlines is one of a very few that list fun as a key value right at the top of their list. Not only do they want their team members to have fun, they are equally focused on bringing that light spirit and fun attitude to their customers. At Southwest this is perhaps the most important WOO to seize every day to generate lasting and extraordinary success. When we lighten up instead of tighten up, like Southwest Airlines, we, too, will soar to new heights.

On an individual level, lightening up when others tighten up can have a truly extraordinary lifelong impact on our family members and even the world around us.

Canadian Nobel Prize–winning physicist Willard Boyle, the inventor of CCD technology, used to create high-quality digital imaging, was once asked about the biggest influence on his life. He spoke without hesitation about his mother and her unusual way of parenting.

As a young boy, one night he had snuck downstairs and gulped down some milk out of the carton. He was old enough to know full well that this was not acceptable in his home. As he reached up to put it back, he spotted his mother watching him. Startled, he dropped the carton, and it broke open, spilling milk everywhere.

But rather than chastising him, his mother kept her cool. She lightened up instead of tightening up. In fact, she turned his misbehavior into a real-life science lesson. She showed her son how the milk flowed into puddles and spread across the floor in a definite pattern. They talked about why drinking from the carton is unsanitary and can spread disease. As they cleaned up the mess she taught him about absorption. All the while she asked him questions that caused him to think. Gently she helped him understand that she didn't want him to repeat this mistake, but even more, she wanted him to learn something from every experience.

Most of us, having caught one of our children red-handed doing something against the rules, would probably have responded with anger and possible punishment. But this mother chose to thrive rather than cry over spilled milk. She looked for the WOO and turned it into a learning situation. That same choice is there for us no matter the circumstances we face.

As leaders, parents, friends, teachers, or mentors, what would our behavior look like if we lightened up instead of tightened up? I believe that we could help replace the fear of failure in others with a passion for learning.

This is an important secret to treating others with dignity and respect. It recognizes that most mistakes are errors of execution rather than intention. Such an understanding helps lighten our spirit so that we interact with others in ways that reinforce our belief in them, and in turn their desire to do the right things and find new solutions.

As the first day of practice began in his senior year at UCLA, three-time All-American Bill Walton, sporting a goatee and bushy red sideburns, stepped forward at the opening team meeting and said to his coach, the legendary John Wooden: "With all due respect, Coach, several of us are seniors now and are over twenty-one. We feel we should be able to have beards or mustaches if we want them."

Coach Wooden, who maintained a no-facial-hair rule for his players, smiled kindly at Walton and approached him, gently patting him on the back. Then, calmly and without a hint of anger or irritation, he said to his star center, in front of the entire team: "Bill, I've never been more proud of you. A man needs to stand up for what he believes. You've grown into a fine leader. And we're really going to miss you!"

Ten minutes later Walton returned from the locker room clean-shaven. His mountain-man beard would have to wait until he turned pro with the Portland Trail Blazers.

Coach Wooden often said that it is important to be able to disagree without being disagreeable. This simple principle enabled him to uphold his convictions, rules, and standards while treating all around him with dignity and respect, from his star players to those who rarely saw game action. To Coach Wooden, discipline is meant to correct and teach, not to punish or demean. And it can be delivered with a light touch rather than a sledgehammer.

I believe showing this kind of respect in the way we deal with our team members during the most challenging times will fuel their desire to learn from their mistakes. Although they always want to perform well and make great decisions, missteps and adversity are sometimes the greatest igniters of new discovery and exciting WOOs.

I work with clients such as Microsoft, Cisco, and Kaiser Permanente, and one of their foremost goals is to create environments that foster healthy risk taking and bold ideas that challenge the status quo. They realize that change is happening so rapidly that if they slow down their efforts to innovate, they are actually going backward. They recognize that in big organizations, the key to flexibility, agility, and opportunity is to build a team of decision makers who are eager to enhance new WOOs. The secret to moving from fear and failure to freedom and faith is to lead with the same bigger-picture perspective so beautifully exemplified by Willard Boyle's mother. Seize the WOO to lighten up rather than tighten up, especially when a little milk is spilled.

A WOO for You

Think of a situation recently in which you became angry or frustrated with a colleague or loved one for making a mistake or not living up to your expectations. Then ask yourself how you could have turned that error or misunderstanding into an opportunity to learn, using your creativity, kindness, and wisdom. How could you have made that learning experience fun and enlightening, a positive pivot point for them as well as you? What would happen if the next time such a WOO arises, you put your new constructive approach right into action by lightening up instead of tightening up?

16

Us Versus Them

Does this sound a bit familiar in your organization? The operations and administrative groups can't stand the sales folks. And sales can't stand operations and administration. How many WOOs are slammed shut because of these kinds of corporate silos, those insidious "us versus them" feuds that erupt within our own teams? How can we bust out of that narrow thinking to ignite upward momentum and synergy wherever we go?

When I was a swimming coach, I became convinced that something magical happened to my swimmers when they competed in relays. Whether they were beginners or swimming at a national level, these young athletes always performed better in relays than individually. Some of my most vivid memories were of relay teammates cheering madly together as the anchor swimmer drove for home. Watching them lean toward the water, completely focused on encouraging their teammates with energy and support, was incredibly inspiring. In those extraordinary moments there was no ego. There was only *we*-go.

When the relay was over, regardless of who touched the

wall first, the entire team embraced each other with unrestrained appreciation. No one cared who swam the fastest leg of the relay. There were no silos, no "me versus you." They were silo-busters who knew that *everyone* was important. They knew that the greatest individual relay leg in history was worth nothing without the rest of the team. It was the total team effort that mattered.

Just like relay teammates, silo-busters in companies view team spirit and mutual support as unconditional. They recognize that when we support only those who are just like us, we build barriers rather than bridges. Silo-busters operate from faith, so there is no separation, prejudice, or exclusion. Dedicated silo-busters cherish differences rather than fear them.

Silos are most often constructed from the unstable building block called comparison. Like asbestos in our bodies, comparison to others can rapidly create a cancer in our business or family. We can tear down our children's spirit and confidence when comparing one to the other in a poorly thought-out attempt to motivate. When we ask with consternation, "Why don't you act more like your sister?" we have set siblings up as rivals, with one the good kid and the other the bad kid. If we don't change that pattern of unnecessary comparison, our children may begin to see themselves in this way.

The WOO opens for us when we realize we don't have to use comparison to help guide and teach. Instead we can simply focus on the child whose behavior we want to improve. We could ask, "How could you have handled this differently?" We could let them know that we believe in them and know they can make a better choice. As we guide them, we build and reinforce their confidence and self-esteem.

In the workplace, comparison is often driven by fear—we fear differences rather than embrace them. Comparison sets up a win-lose scenario. Real success, teamwork, and momentum come only from win-win.

When I became the vice president of marketing and sales for a major transportation company headquartered in Seattle, I initially had an extremely difficult time connecting with the vice president of operations. When I looked at him all I could see were our differences. He had a serious, focused demeanor and was extremely deliberate and analytical. I was much more playful, quicker to make decisions, and very upbeat. For all my positivity, my focus on our differences in style and personality had a very negative effect upon our company. It created a separation between our functional areas that kept us from performing at the highest possible level.

One morning I finally decided that if things were to change, I must change. I walked around the corner to his office and sat down to talk with no real agenda other than to get to know him better and to simply be present with him. Soon we were talking about our families, about our endurance training (I was running marathons at that time and he was an avid long-distance bicyclist), and finally about how passionate we were about the people in our company and our desire to deliver exceptional value to our customers. I walked out of his office with an epiphany: he cared about our team every bit as much as I did.

It was only when I looked beyond our differences that I could see how much we had in common. And when I realized that we shared the most important goals and inspiration for our company, it opened my eyes to the value his different approach, talents, and experience brought to the team. His analytical approach zeroed in on details that could have impacted us negatively and which I probably would have missed. From that day on we never held a major sales and marketing meeting without our mutual collaboration.

Spurred by our new appreciation for each other and for our different, complementary approaches, our company achieved extraordinary results. We were recognized in our industry's top publication as the best in our field for customer service and convenience. We added jobs and our revenues and profits soared. Our company became innovative, agile, and, most of all, an exceptional place to work. By valuing our differences, he and I seized a WOO that made a lasting difference for every employee, for their families, and for our customers.

That experience changed the way I look at differences. I don't want to have on my team only people who see the world just as I do, because then we'll see only what I see. I want people around me who see the things I miss, who have passion and talent in areas that I lack. Through our collaboration, we can create extraordinary results.

I am known as "America's Breakthrough Coach" because I have had nearly half a million participants in my seminars over the past twenty-five years break through wooden boards karate style. I have everyone write down on the front of their boards a fear, limit, obstacle, or doubt they are determined to break through in their lives. On the other side of the board I instruct them to write down what's waiting for them when they have broken through—what they are going to feel, be, have, and create in their lives because they have moved beyond the obstacle.

The secret to breaking through the board is to focus beyond the obstacle, to look beyond the board. In real life, often the most challenging "boards" to break through are differences. They can become like solar eclipses, blocking out all the light. When we embrace and appreciate each other's differences, we can open some of the most fulfilling, rich, and life-changing WOOs of all.

My wife, Carole, is different from me in many ways. She is at ease at parties and social events even when we hardly know anyone there. I am awkward and anxious from the moment we receive the invitation to attend. Our energies are reversed when it comes to public speaking, where I am in my element and she must summon her inner courage. Carole has studied natural health and nutrition for thirty years. Before I met her, my idea of healthy eating was being sure I ate my pickle with my double cheeseburger and fries. I have an unstoppable belief in prosperity, while Carole grew up in a very frugal family that worried constantly about money. Because we have learned to see the beauty in our differences, these polar opposites have strengthened our marriage and deepened our love. In fact, it is because of these differences that Carole has been my greatest teacher and helped me grow in ways I never would have thought possible.

By learning to be unafraid of our differences in style, approach, and talents, we have been able to look more deeply and build a life together centered upon the truly important things we have in common: our passion for family and for filling our home with love and light; our love of learning and belief that we can change for the better; and our belief in kindness, compassion, humility, and, above all, love. We may not be like-minded about everything, but we are like-hearted in our highest values and in the ways that matter most.

Seeing the value in our differences is a clear indicator that we believe in abundance rather than scarcity. It allows us to replace fear and distrust in the face of differences with curiosity, interest, and above all, compassion. By seeking to understand other people's differences we expand our thinking, heighten our awareness, and truly grow. We turn "us versus them" into "we," and silos into synergy.

A WOO for You

What would changing the way you value differences mean to you? Why not set up a WOO by arranging to sit down with someone in your personal life or career whose differences have impacted the way you've interacted with each other? Encourage them to tell you their personal story, their greatest influences, experiences, teachers, and breakthroughs. Ask them about what's most important to them and what has made them most proud in life. As St. Francis of Assisi and Stephen Covey so powerfully taught, seek to understand before seeking to be understood. Then you could ask yourself how your differences in style, demeanor, approach, and talents could work together to strengthen your relationship and create a better team.

A Bonus WOO for You

Every morning as I arise I repeat St. Francis of Assisi's powerful Prayer for Peace. It has become a practice that opens my spirit to value differences, and to approach each day and every challenge with compassion and kindness. I offer it to you with the hope that it will lift each day for you as it does for me, to view everyone you meet as teammates on a lifelong relay of understanding and tolerance.

> Dear Lord, please make me an instrument of your peace.
> Where there is hatred, let me sow love.
> Where there is injury, pardon.
> Where there is doubt, faith.
> Where there is despair, hope.
> Where there is darkness, light.
> And where there is sadness, joy.

Divine Master, please grant that I may not so much seek to be consoled as to console.
To be understood as to understand.
To be loved as to love.
For it is in giving that we receive.
It is in pardoning that we are pardoned.
And it is in dying that we are born to eternal life.

17

Pesky Need for Approval!

In the early days of my professional speaking career I would rush off to some quiet corner as soon as the seminar ended to read through every single evaluation. In fact, I devoured them. What was I looking for? As ridiculous as it now seems to me, I was obsessed with the desire for everyone in the event to give me perfect scores. In a word, what I so desperately craved was *perfection*; what I wanted was their absolute approval. It didn't matter if 99 percent of the participants had loved me. All I saw was the one percent who didn't give me glowing approval. Anything less than 100 percent validation left me feeling crushed and completely rejected.

One day after a seminar in St. Louis I finally broke through. As I tore into the evaluations like an addict needing a fix, a question popped into my mind that transformed my thinking: *Why am I doing this work?* Instantly the light came on. I realized that I loved speaking not because of the response and approval but rather because of the way I felt when I was presenting to an eager audience. I was doing exactly the work I was put on this earth to do.

After that I never asked for evaluations again. I replaced the need for approval with simple gratitude. By letting go of the need for approval I have felt more energy, inspiration, and joy in my work for well over twenty years.

The need for approval can never be satisfied. And as long as it holds sway, it tears down our confidence, energy, and performance. We give up our power to a despot who can never get enough.

But there's good news! No matter how long we have tormented ourselves with our insatiable need for approval, we can let it go. How? First by becoming aware that it is a thirst that can never be quenched, and by replacing that dependence with gratitude.

What happens when we let go of the need for approval? As we release our crippling dependence we stop comparing ourselves to others and obsessing over our need to prove ourselves in whatever we do. We stop worrying about what everybody else thinks about us, and free ourselves to enjoy who we really are. It's amazing what can be accomplished when no one cares who gets the credit.

In my seminars, after we have talked about the 10-point energy scale, participants often ask me a question that cuts right to the heart of the paralyzing impact of our need for approval. They tell me that they have plenty of energy most of the time and with most people. But, they ask me, what should they do about the one person in their life who seems to literally suck the energy right out of them? Often it is someone who is very important in their life: a parent, partner, spouse, boss, or colleague.

My two-word answer is always the same: "Stop it!"

I go on to explain to the participants that no one can take their energy or spirit away without their permission. They have been *giving* it away because of their need for approval. I encourage them to take their energy back. The solution is not to change others, but rather to change themselves. It is remarkable how often seizing this WOO to reclaim their energy and let go of the need for approval leads to much-improved relationships, confidence, and peace of mind.

When I was a boy, my dad was my hero. No one could dislodge my father from the top of my list. As I grew up he was all the things I believed a man was supposed to be: honest, humble, hardworking, tough, and strong. More than anything on this earth I wanted my dad's approval and admiration. I wanted to hear him tell me that I was special. I wanted him to hug me. Most of all I wanted to know that he loved me.

But my dad could not do those things. He had grown up in an era when men were taught to be strong and silent. His father was a brilliant physician, but very serious and no-nonsense. So Dad was raised with very little praise and a great emphasis on figuring things out for himself and never complaining. He valued humility, self-discipline, independence, and mental toughness.

As I grew older, subconsciously I thought that if I could be great at something, then my big, strong dad would tell me he loved me. So I began to work hard in school and sports, hoping that by excelling I could finally receive his admiration and praise. But the more I achieved, the more elusive his respect seemed to become. If I brought home a report card with all A's and one A-minus, he'd quietly look it over and then ask me what I had done wrong in that one subject. If I won four gold medals and a bronze at a swimming meet, he'd ask why I hadn't worked harder in the event where I came in third.

I didn't realize it at the time, but my dad was trying his best to keep me from having a huge ego, from being conceited and arrogant. He figured I received lots of praise from everywhere else, from my teachers and coaches, so he needed to be the one to keep me in line. He also wanted me to never settle for anything less than my best.

But none of that occurred to me. I just felt that I was never quite good enough. And so the need for approval became the subconscious driving force in my life.

On the outside it seemed that this relentless drive was producing good results. My grades were excellent, I was elected president of my high school class, and I excelled in athletics. I was accepted into Stanford and graduated with honors.

But on the inside I was a mess. The more I accomplished, the more I feared I wouldn't do as well the next time. The more my friends loved and appreciated me, the less I felt their love and appreciation. I locked myself in my comfort zones, terrified of adventure and new challenges. Potential WOOs were blocked from my vision by my fear that others would see that I really didn't measure up.

During those years I distanced myself from my dad. I pretended that his love and approval didn't really matter to me. But I was lying to myself. I wanted him to tell me he loved me and that he was proud of me just as much as that little boy who idolized him had wanted it.

One day when my fear of not being good enough almost swallowed me, I realized that my need for approval was destroying my confidence, energy, and spirit. It finally hit me that I had been desperately trying to be the best at whatever I did and that it was never enough. My life pivoted around a single word. I stopped my impossible obsession with trying to be *the* best and for the first time allowed myself to find joy in simply being *my* best.

With that simple shift I began to find peace. I could laugh at myself again, and gradually I let go of the need to compare myself to others. Like magic, WOOs of the greatest magnitude began to appear. I met Carole and for the first time in my life built a relationship based upon honesty and trust. I wanted her to know me for who I really was, to see my weaknesses, not just my strengths. I loved her even more than I wanted her love.

One of the most wonderful of all outcomes from letting go of the need for approval has been the change in my relationship with my dad. I can't even begin to describe how much it means to me that today he is my friend. We enjoy each other's company and laugh easily together. When I'm with him I no longer feel that I have anything to prove. And I love and admire him more than ever.

Perhaps most remarkable of all, as I learned to let go of the need for my dad's approval I discovered that he had been giving it to me all along. He could never say he loved me, but he worked two jobs, sixteen hours a day, all the years I was growing up so we would have a good home. He couldn't give me a hug, but he spent hours and hours rebuilding an old bicycle and turning it into one of the coolest Christmas presents I've ever received. He couldn't tell me he was proud of me, but he told everybody else.

When we are ruled by the need for approval, we can't see it when it's already there right in front of us. Today my dad is still my hero, but I don't need his love and approval. I had it all along.

A WOO for You

How would it feel for you to let go of your need for approval? What would the impact be on your career and your relationships if you could learn to be less dependent upon what others think of you and more inspired by how great it feels to know you're giving the best you're capable of? If you have an "energy vampire" in your life, isn't it time to joyfully reclaim your energy? You no longer need to try to impress them or to give up your power to them. After all, it's not their energy, it's *yours*. Releasing your energy vampire need not be an act of angry defiance. It can be joyful and motivated by gratitude. Like my dad did for me, your energy vampire has provided you with a magnificent WOO. They've challenged you to see that no one can dampen your spirit, stifle your confidence, or damage your peace of mind unless you give them permission. By reclaiming your energy you will take a giant step toward freeing yourself from the need for approval.

18

You'll Be Amazed at What You Can Do When You Seize the WOO!

Several years ago, my friend John Locke approached me with an idea that we both immediately saw as a WOO. John is a highly decorated Toastmaster and a huge fan of personal development and team building as accelerators of business success. He had hired me to speak at a couple of events for companies he had worked for over the years, and he knew that not only did I share that belief but that it was my passion and purpose. We were avid believers in the catalytic power of live events to ignite innovation, energy, and excellence. We both love living in the city of Asheville, North Carolina, and felt that with its vitality and openness as a community that has drawn so many artists, authors, and small-business entrepreneurs, our home had the potential to become a pacesetter in the areas of personal and professional growth.

The challenge was that small businesses and sole proprietors lacked the resources to hire top speakers and thought leaders for live events. Virtually all of my professional speaking events are backed by larger companies, so I rarely ever have the opportunity to deliver my presentations to small businesses or to individuals.

John's vision was to organize an event where these small-business owners, entrepreneurs, and teachers—so much the very heart of our community—would have the chance to attend a program normally available only to larger organizations with sizable training budgets. His vision inspired me, and by the time we finished our lunch meeting I had volunteered to donate my services as the keynote speaker at the event. We decided to make the event truly affordable by charging only twenty dollars per attendee. We hoped to attract a hundred participants. We would promote the event solely through our own personal networks and word of mouth, since our advertising budget was zero. I offered to give the first sixty-four enrollees a copy of my book *Beyond Success*, hoping that the extra incentive would help us pull this off. We even came up with a name: Lessons in Leadership.

John, the master networker (see Chapter 10), realized that to fulfill this vision we would need a venue, a website, and a small team. He approached a friend, Bill Kelley, who was a leader at the Grove Park Inn, a grand Asheville hotel. Bill jumped at the idea of making a real difference in our community, and a couple of days later he came back to us and told us he had reserved a beautiful ballroom for no charge—and the audiovisual equipment and manpower would be donated as well!

In conversations with two special friends, Keith Challenger, a marketing wizard and VP of a healthcare company in the area, and Dana Stonestreet, the president of HomeTrust Bank, John described the Lessons in Leadership vision. Keith and Dana both immediately stepped forward and volunteered to be a part of the team.

The event would be in late January, which gave us about twelve weeks to put the entire thing together. It also meant that much of our promotional period would fall right smack in the heart of the holiday season. But our fearless team of five dived in full bore with unabashed enthusiasm.

It's amazing what can be accomplished when no one cares who gets the credit. I had never been a part of a more selfless, energized, and egoless team. Whoever was best equipped to handle each task simply stepped up and did it, with passion and purpose. Our meetings were great fun and remarkably efficient. We all saw Lessons in Leadership as a gift to the community we loved. Whatever we could contribute to transform that vision into reality was a joy, not a job.

In the end, six hundred people participated in that first Lessons in Leadership session. Bill Kelley delivered an inspiring opening presentation on service excellence, and I followed with my "Breakthrough Leadership" keynote. The ballroom was filled with small-business owners, teachers, students, entrepreneurs, and individuals with a desire to grow. Over the next seven years Lessons in Leadership became one of the most successful events in Asheville. We held firm to the $20 price and saw the event grow to nearly two thousand participants. Speakers such as Bob Proctor, Dr. Nido Qubein, and Harry Paul donated their services. (When I approached these top speakers about Lessons in Leadership, I asked if they believed in free speech. When they said "Of course," I cracked them up when I followed with, "Great! Because this is definitely a *free* speech!")

The success of the event created an interesting dilemma for us. We had hoped we could break even when we held the first event. But suddenly we had thousands of dollars of profit. So since we had established Lessons in Leadership as a gift to the community, we decided to give all the money to local charities. Over the years we have donated more than $60,000, which provided forty thousand meals through Manna Food Bank, helped fund programs for children and seniors through the YMCA, and made a real difference in Asheville. We were able to offer scholarships to the events for disadvantaged youth and expose them to ideas and principles that we hoped would ignite their lives.

When you are open to WOOs in your life, eager to disrupt the status quo, even seemingly small ideas can lead to breakthrough results. In 2007 Brian Chesky and Joe Gebbia couldn't afford to pay the rent for their San Francisco apartment. More out of desperation than inspiration, they decided to try to rent out the loft space in the apartment; they offered three air mattresses and a hot breakfast for $80 a person. They knew that hotel space in downtown San Francisco was hard to come by and expensive; especially when big events were taking place around the city. They designed a very basic website and called their little enterprise Airbed & Breakfast. Their first three guests stayed for several days each, and suddenly Brian and Joe could make their rent payment.

That little spark of success caused Brian and Joe to ask themselves what if there were others who wanted to do the same. They offered to promote other people's rentals for them on their Airbed & Breakfast site for a one-time membership fee.

At first the idea caught on rather slowly, and Brian and Joe plus their techie buddy Nathan Blecharczyk, whom they'd convinced to come aboard and take over the web design and technical operations, sank what little income they generated back into the business. By mid-2008 they realized that if things didn't pick up soon they would have to give up on the idea. With the presidential election campaign in full swing and the Democratic National Convention coming to San Francisco, they hit upon a playful idea to try to raise seed funds. They purchased hundreds of boxes of cereal and designed box covers spotlighting caricatures of the candidates, including "Obama O's" and "Cap'n McCain's." They generated $30,000 from the sales of these collectable cereal boxes, which kept them in business and their vision alive.

But still their growth was slow. They were barely scraping by and getting very tired of living on a diet of cereal! Finally they decided they had to try something different if they wanted to bring new energy into their enterprise. They flew to New York City and went door to door to see how their newly renamed Airbnb really worked for their host partners. During these on-site visits it struck them that the photos of the locations their hosts offered that were posted on the Airbnb website were generally poor in quality. So they hired a photographer and tested the rental activity these professional shots generated. Very quickly they found that the professional photos boosted booking sharply, as much as three times more compared to their previous listings. When they provided this professional photo service to their hosts, their business began to take off.

In 2009 they began to collect a small fee from both the renters and the hosts for managing and marketing the lodging transaction. The entire process was operated digitally online, with payments to hosts made via automatic drafts into their accounts. In 2010 they grew by more than 800 percent, flew past the one-million-nights-booked mark, and offered Airbnb in more than thirty countries, sparking serious interest from major investors. They were on their way.

Today Airbnb is available in nearly two hundred countries

around the world and offers more than one and a half million rooms each night, far more than any hotel chain. They have been a major player in sparking a new model of the way the world does business, called the sharing economy. Though they face challenges from the hospitality industry and some local governments, they have disrupted the status quo and revolutionized the way millions of people look for lodging. It's amazing what you can do when you seize the WOO!

When my younger daughter, Jenna, was attending the University of Georgia, during her last two years, from 2012 to 2014, I noticed occasional expenditures for something called Uber on her bank statement each month. My initial thought was that Uber must be a café, or perhaps a tanning salon or yoga studio. When I finally asked her about Uber, she explained that it was a ride service that was really easy, safe, and affordable, even for college students.

Jenna eventually convinced me to actually give Uber a try when I traveled for my speaking engagements, and I quickly became a dedicated fan and regular patron. I marveled at the beautiful simplicity of the concept and how it managed to address every frustrating and inadequate element of typical taxi service and replace it with the ideal solution.

I remembered many cab rides where the payment transaction had turned into an ordeal; either they didn't accept credit cards or the card processing machine was malfunctioning or incredibly slow. It was uncanny how this always seemed to happen when I was in a rush to make a flight or get to a meeting. And how often had taxi drivers pulled up in cabs that reeked of cigarette smoke, blasted music when I was trying to make phone calls, or turned on the air-conditioning only if the temperature soared to about 110 degrees? I thought of how often

I had been amazed that my cab driver did not have a GPS and it had fallen to me to tell the driver how to get to my destination, even if I'd been to that city only three times in my life. Certainly I had many excellent drivers and enjoyable cab rides over the years, but the inconsistency and consequent sense that I was rolling the dice hoping for a good experience every time I hailed a taxi was unsettling.

Uber simply and effectively disrupted this less-than-satisfying status quo to provide a service that was easy, consistent, and technologically savvy, and that gave both the passenger and the driver the opportunity to give immediate and direct feedback about the experience. Uber gave me the feeling of choice, control, and confidence.

I could see when and where my driver was approaching, could speak with them and see the history of their service performance, and know the approximate cost of my ride before I agreed to step into their vehicle (which, by the way, was always clean, neat, and comfortable). The payment transaction was automatic, requiring absolutely no time, because all the necessary information was already in place from when I'd first entered it after installing the Uber application on my phone. No longer would I lose half my tiny cab receipts, because with Uber the receipts are instantly sent to my email.

Uber reminds me of the genius who finally figured out that we really didn't have to lug heavy suitcases and could actually attach wheels to them so they could roll. How many millions of us just accepted that it was natural for our right arm to be longer than our left as a result of toting these bulging bags until someone finally stopped looking at what was and instead envisioned what could be?

In a little over five years Uber zoomed from start-up to a

company valued in excess of $17 billion, providing employment and additional income to hundreds of thousands while radically elevating the quality of ride service. They have changed the world by seizing the WOO.

Like Airbnb, Uber is facing challenges as they chart this new course. The taxi industry has been hit hard by the skyrocketing success of Uber and must make very significant changes to compete. Uber is also dealing with legal questions about whether their workforce of contract drivers is entitled to employee rights and benefits. But even as they navigate these challenges and issues, Uber continues to grow at a staggering pace and to become the top-of-mind choice for ride service, particularly with millennials and Gen Xers. They see themselves not as a transportation company but as a technology company and are investing billions of dollars into developing systems and technological advancements that will impact industries well beyond their own. The window of opportunity to change the world opens only when we refuse to use our memory to see.

Just as Airbnb and Uber are vivid examples in business of the extraordinary possibilities that abound when we disrupt the status quo and break through comfort zones that have become confinement zones, my friend Meridith Elliott Powell is a brilliant example of what we can accomplish and become when we break through from the woe to the WOO.

Meridith is one of the top business speakers in the nation on sales, personal responsibility, and developing women leaders in today's economy. The instant you meet Meridith your spirit soars. You can't help but trust her and admire her dy-

namic energy. Instead of being overpowering, she is empowering, with a contagious smile and a passion for life. She simply
makes you feel good about yourself.

It's hard to imagine that as a young woman she suffered
from deep depression and a self-image so damaged that she
thought of taking her own life on several occasions. Her father
died from alcoholism when she was a teenager, and addiction
seemed to follow her wherever she went: she married an al-
coholic when she was quite young. Though she never fell into
substance addiction herself, she was in a very real sense ad-
dicted to addiction. She was an enabler who felt deep down
that the life she had created as the daughter and wife of serious addicts was exactly the life she deserved. When after a few
years of marriage her husband died from his addictions, she
sank deeper into darkness.

So how did Meridith get from there to where she is today?
How did she transform herself from tragedy to triumph, from
fear to freedom? How did she change her life?

She did it the same way my friend Tom did through his
Year of the Tom. She did it the same way the remarkable young
woman in my seminar did after she lost her legs. She did it
in exactly the same way that my swimmer Ron did when he
soared to heights we'd never even dreamed of. She did it the
same way Uber and Airbnb have transformed the way we do
business and the way Kaiser Permanente rose from worst to
first. She did it the way we all can do it, and the only way we've
ever done it: by making one pivotal choice that was available to
her, just as it's always available to all of us. She shifted her focus
from her fears, obstacles, and doubts to the WOO.

So now it's your turn. Open your eyes and heart to the windows of opportunity in your family, your business, and your

community. Let in that fresh light every single day. Disrupt the status quo and begin to use your vision rather than your memory to see. Most of all open the windows of opportunity that are already there in front of you. When you change the way you look at yourself, the self you see will change, too. You'll be amazed at what you can do when you seize the WOO.

ACKNOWLEDGMENTS

I believe that the greatest of all emotions is gratitude, and I am overflowing with thankfulness to so many remarkable friends and colleagues for their help, guidance, creativity, and unending support in making *There Are No Overachievers* come to life. First and foremost, I thank my wife, Carole, daughters Kelsey and Jenna, and son-in-law, Michael, for inspiring me every single day. My mother and father, Miriam and Lou Biro, and my sister, Katlin Hecox, are the greatest examples of energy, responsibility, work ethic, and honesty I have ever known. I love you very much.

My tremendous friends Blaine and Cynthia Greenfield, Tom and Marcy Gallagher, Marvin Sadovsky, Annemarie Brown, Sunny Ruble, and Bonnie Sibner—collectively known as my "framily"—ignite my heart and spirit more than they could ever know. I thank John Locke, the greatest networker I've ever met, for his example of unselfishness and simple human kindness. To Meridith Elliott Powell for being a model of resilience and transformation, I extend unending appreciation. My partners at AVANOO—Daniel Jacobs, Prosper Nwankpa, and Elise

Otalora—fire up my creative spirit and challenge me to grow each and every day.

I am so inspired by the teams at Southwest Airlines, Kaiser Permanente, Airbnb, Uber, and WestJet for being magnificent models of the Window of Opportunity spirit.

Keith Challenger—Sir Keith—your brilliance and constant unconditional support are simply astonishing.

Like Lou Gehrig, I feel like "the luckiest man on the face of the earth" to be guided by my fantastic editor, Roger Scholl, and the extraordinary team at Crown Business. You are simply the BEST!

And finally to Margret McBride and Faye Atchison at the McBride Literary Agency: without your wisdom, insight, and most of all, faith, this book would never have been completed. As a man known to "cry at openings of supermarkets," I find myself choking up with gratitude for all you've done for me. Thank you for helping me let every reader discover that there is more in them than they ever dreamed possible.

INDEX

Index

ABOUT THE AUTHOR

Author of the bestseller *Beyond Success*, BRIAN BIRO was the number 1 speaker at four consecutive *Inc.* magazine international conferences. Biro has appeared on *Good Morning America*, CNN, Fox, and as a featured speaker at the Disney Institute in Orlando. Biro was recently named one of the top one hundred most inspirational graduates of the UCLA Graduate School of Business.